A Lord Mayor
in Wartime Norwich

Arthur John Cleveland

Lord Mayor of Norwich
from 9th November 1942 to 8th November 1943.

A Lord Mayor's Year
in Wartime Norwich

ISBN 978-1-9993672-3-7

British Library Cataloguing-in-Publication Data
A catalogue record for this book is available from the British Library

Designed by
Charlotte Cleveland

Printed in Great Britain by The Lavenham Press Ltd.

Acknowledgements

Much information and most of the illustrations come from the Cleveland family papers, scrapbooks, and photographic albums etc. I would like to thank for additional help the Norfolk Heritage Centre at The Forum in Norwich, Judy Ball, Jane Blanchflower, Christine Cleveland, Katharine Clayton, Sir Timothy Colman, Rosemary Dixon, Lizzy Lloyd, Bob Malster, *Eastern Daily Press* and Archant.

Also by David Cleveland:
East Anglia on Film. 1987 (Poppyland Publishing)
Manningtree and Mistley – the people, the trades, and the industries. 2007. 2nd edition 2012
Manningtree Station. 2008
Films Were Made Volume 1 The Region at Work – A look at films and film makers in the East of England. 2009
Films Were Made Volume 2 Local History - A look at films and film makers in the East of England. 2011
Lightships off the Essex Coast and the Story of LV 18. 2012
How Films Were Made and Shown. 2015
Let's Go To The Pictures. 2018
Southwold Picture Palace. 2019
A Look Back at The Broads. 2019

Also published by David Cleveland:
Stour Secrets by Ken Rickwood 2008
Stour Odyssey by Ken Rickwood 2010
The Colne by Ken Rickwood 2013
Colchester's Secret Roman River by Ken Rickwood. 2019
A Hickling Marshman's Diary by Gerald Nudd. 2019

Front cover picture
The Lord Mayor, Arthur Cleveland, inspecting the works fire brigade of Boulton and Paul, Riverside Works, Norwich on Friday 5th March 1943.

The announcement on Thursday 24th September 1942 in the Eastern Daily Press *of Norwich's Lord Mayor designate. Dr. Arthur Cleveland officially became Lord Mayor on 9th November that year. The EDP, as it was affectionately known, was published and printed by the Norfolk News Co. of 57 London Street, Norwich.*

Introduction

The front page of the *Eastern Daily Press* of Thursday 24th September 1942 carried the headlines 'Russian Pressure At Stalingrad', 'British in 500-Mile Raid' and 'Madagascar - British Occupy The Capital' left no one in doubt of the intensity of war. In the middle of all this was a piece headed 'The Lord Mayor Designate'.

Under two photographs was the caption 'Dr. Arthur J. Cleveland, who is to be the next Lord Mayor of Norwich, and Mrs. Cleveland. Portraits of Mr. John Brooksbank, the Sheriff Designate, and Mrs. Brooksbank, will be found on page 3'.

1

The Sheriff Designate, Mr. John Brooksbank, and Mrs. Brooksbank, as printed on page 3 of the Eastern Daily Press *on 24th September 1942.*

Inside an article said "The choice of Lord Mayor this time falls to the Conservative Party, but Dr. Cleveland would be the first to admit that in him is little of the politician, and this will be his first association with civic affairs. He has, however, already rendered city and county inestimable service in his long connexion with the Norfolk and Norwich Hospital, both as a physician and its management."

But it was only September 1942, and John Barnes was still in office as Lord Mayor of Norwich (before that he had been on the Council for 25 years) with Clifford White as Sheriff. The new Mayor would not take over until 9th November.

Dr. Arthur John Cleveland (1872-1957) was the only Lord Mayor of that time not to be an Alderman or connected to Norwich City Council in any way. In those days it was possible for a well known person in the city to be voted to this civic office.

Arthur Cleveland was born in Brighton on 17th September 1872, the youngest son of Henry Cleveland, solicitor to the Government in Bombay. Henry Cleveland's father, William, owned fishing boats and property at Lowestoft and was described after his death in 1862 as a 'gentleman'.

Arthur Cleveland first encountered Norfolk at an early age when living at Long Stratton in the home of Dr. Thomas Barton until his parents returned from India. After attending various schools, including Clifton College near Bristol, he received his medical training at Guy's Hospital in London, where he qualified in 1897. He became a house physician and between 1899 and 1901 was medical registrar and tutor.

He married Evelyn Jackson of London in 1900 and, after a trip to India, moved to Norwich in 1902 living at first at No.4 Thorpe Road, and listed in *Jarrolds Norwich Directory* of that year as 'Cleveland, A. J. M.D., M.R.C.P., Surgeon'. They had a son, John Cleveland (1902-1971), who from 1927 farmed at Horstead, and a daughter Geraldine Cleveland (1904-1992), known as Deenie, who we shall hear more from later.

The medical staff of the Norfolk and Norwich Hospital in 1906.
Arthur John Cleveland is the tall one in the back row standing
fourth from the left.

Arthur John Cleveland is listed in year-by-year directories as living at 8 Thorpe Road in 1904, 10 Thorpe Road in 1908, 4 Thorpe Road in 1911, and 13 Thorpe Road in 1913. The reason for these variations in the directories may have been a mixture of rented homes (he never bought a property) and his consulting rooms.

Arthur Cleveland became electrotherapeutist and radiologist at the Norfolk and Norwich Hospital in 1904, and assistant physician in 1906. In that year he was also appointed physician to the Jenny Lind Infirmary For Children, and later consulting physician to the Norwich City Hospital in Bowthorpe Road. He became secretary of the Norwich Medico-Chirurgical Society [of doctors and surgeons] in 1907. He was also President in 1924.

He was one of the first to use an X-ray machine. His son, John Cleveland, who was born in their home in Thorpe Mansions in Thorpe Road in 1902, recalled that his father was "the first doctor to use X -Ray in Norwich in those days and had a massive piece of such equipment installed in his consulting room. He was a man not renowned for the evenness of his temper and I remember seeing sparks flying out of it once while father fiddled with it while calling it various names.

"We moved a little further up the road to a larger house and that was where we were when the First World War started. My father then became a Major in the R.A.M.C. [Royal Army Medical Corps] and was stationed at Thorpe Hospital. I can remember the black out and standing outside the back door listening to the hum of the Zeppelins overhead. Those were grim days with little food and a terrible loss of life. Poor father used to get so upset when the trainloads of wounded arrived at Thorpe Station on route for the hospital."

Arthur Cleveland's hobbies were woodwork, golf, fly fishing and reading. John, his son, remembered helping his father with his carpentry. "He was a Doctor of Medicine and an extremely well read man but he loved to make things of wood. I got a bit bored holding the nails once while he built a summer house, but I learnt a great deal also. How to make joints and use triangular construction and how to handle tools."

Occasionally the family would go to the seaside; nearly always Newport near Hemsby, where Arthur Cleveland would say the day was ruined if other people were in sight on the beach. Another hobby was shooting as his son recalled. "I can remember learning to shoot with my father in the woods and on the marshes at Postwick. One day when in a thick wood I shot at a rabbit, missed and heard a loud human cry from not far away. I was panic stricken. What on earth had I done? It soon transpired that unknown to either of us, another doctor had gone into the wood with a gun, and a pellet from my shot at the rabbit head ricocheted off the ground and pierced his lip and landed up against his front teeth! Not too bad and I was let off with a lecture.

"My father was mad about golf and we played a great deal together. The trouble was that neither of us was very good. His handicap was ten and mine twelve. In those days a set of matched clubs was unknown. I played with anything I could lay my hands upon, I had little pocket money left for the vacations. Father used to set out with high spirits confident that he was going to have a first class round. However most times he cracked sooner or later and we would return home dejected. After a drink and a meal he began to become more cheerful and would start to analyse what had gone wrong. So next time we would set out full of hope but generally with the same result.

"I remember how my mother used to play the piano in the evenings when I was lying in bed and how lovely it was. She occasionally played at concerts held in St. Andrews Hall, Norwich, and in the evenings at home friends used to come to hear her play Chopin, Grieg, Liszt etc."

Arthur Cleveland did valuable work at Thorpe Hospital for the military patients there during the First World War for which he was awarded an O.B.E. He had a special interest in neurology and dermatology and was elected F.R.C.P. [Fellow of the Royal College of Physicians] in 1921.

He was an early user of the motor car to get to patients - turning out day or night when the call came. His telephone number was Norwich 68. Later, when telephones were commonplace, it lengthened to 20068. This was a time when doctors were in private practice, well before the National Health Service. John Cleveland said "heaven knows how many patients he treated without being paid. He loved his work and money was only secondary."

Where he was living and his consulting rooms again seems mixed up in the 1920s, for he is listed as at *Fernhill*, Unthank Road in 1924; 224 Unthank Road in 1925 and 1927, and there and at 20 Thorpe Road in 1929.

It seems he was at *Fernhill* in Unthank Road until 1931 when the family was listed as at 33 The Close. For reasons unknown, they stayed there for only four years and then moved next door - to No 34. This remained their home until the late 1950s.

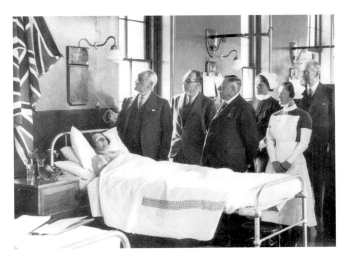

Unveiling a plaque in the Norfolk and Norwich Hospital recording the 'Snapdragon Bed' which was endowed by the Norwich Hospital Annual *in 1930, the year it was first published. £1000 was raised. There were fifteen endowed beds including 'Jeremiah Woodrow' by Mrs. Pilling who gave £1000 in memory of her father in 1916, and 'The Druids Bed' by the Ancient Order of Druids of East Anglia by means of a tinfoil collection which raised £1000 in 1926. In the 1930 picture above Arthur Cleveland is on the right. Snapdragon was a large model of a dragon carried by a man inside at processions and pageants in Norwich mainly up until the 1930s. Its origins were the Guild Day festivities often connected with Mayor Making.*

Queen Elizabeth opened a new maternity wing at the Norfolk and Norwich Hospital on Saturday 29th October 1938. Dr. Cleveland, Chairman of the Board of Management of the hospital between 1938 and 1943, is in the middle of the group.

On Saturday 29th October 1938 Arthur Cleveland showed the Queen round the Norfolk and Norwich Hospital where she opened the new maternity wing which was a memorial to Captain Geoffrey Colman. This official Norwich visit by King George VI and Queen Elizabeth was to celebrate the opening of the new City Hall. The King made a speech from the balcony and in the afternoon went to Carrow Road to watch part of a football match of Norwich playing Millwall.

Between 1937 and 1943 Arthur Cleveland was a Trustee of the Great Hospital in Bishopgate Street. Dr. A. Batty-Shaw, who worked with Arthur Cleveland, described him as "A tall man gifted with a logical brain and with self-confessed streaks of laziness and impatience. He did a great deal for the hospital through his services in committees and administration. For many years on the Board of Management, he was its chairman from 1938-1943, and was always insistent on the influence which the medical staff should have on hospital policy."

Arthur Cleveland and his wife Evelyn lived a sort of Edwardian life style at 34 The Close, with a cook, Mrs. Perry, who came in daily and lived in Anchor Street [no longer in existence – formerly off Barrack Street]; and what may be called a house-maid who lived in a room on the top floor. She was responsible for all other aspects of the house, such as the fires, washing, bedrooms, cleaning etc. During the war years this 'domestic servant' as she was called on the 1939 census was Mary Dack. Then there was Miss Forder, and latterly a Miss Eglington.

Arthur Cleveland liked his meals on time - lunch at 1 o'clock, and if at home afternoon tea at 4.30 often with anchovy paste on toast, and in the evening a meal at 7.30pm. In fact there was a gong in the hall which was banged if he and his wife were in other parts of the house. He occasionally had wine with his meal, and afterwards smoked a Player's Weights cigarette and enjoyed a small bar of Bourneville chocolate. He read the local paper, *The Times* and *Punch*.

The house in the Cathedral Close was rented from the Dean and Chapter - Arthur Cleveland never bought a property in his life. He did have a car though, kept in a garage down by Pulls Ferry. He was still working when he became Lord Mayor, even though at the time he was 70 years old.

On becoming Lord Mayor he was mentioned in the 1943 *Norwich Annual* describing him as "Consulting Physician; Chairman of the Board of Management of the Norfolk and Norwich Hospital; Consulting Neurologist to the Ministries of Health and Pensions, and Medical Referee for County Court Circuit 12; Director of the Norwich Union Life Insurance Society." In 1943 he was also invited to join the board of the Norwich Union Fire Office.

*Norwich Market Place, Guildhall, and the new City Hall
which was opened on 29th October 1938 by King George VI.*

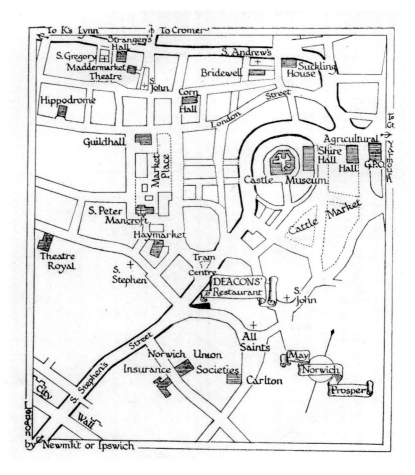

A pre-war map of part of Norwich. Deacons was a
restaurant on the corner of Westlegate and Red Lion Street.

The Norfolk and Norwich Hospital as it was in St. Stephens Road, Norwich.

Setting the Scene

Arthur Cleveland wrote of World War II in his book *A History of the Norfolk and Norwich Hospital* published in 1948 that "Probably the first indications to civilians in Norwich that the danger existed were the inauguration of the Observer Corps in Norfolk in 1934. In November 1935 the Medical Officer of Health for Norwich, acting on instructions from the Government, asked the Norfolk and Norwich and Jenny Lind [children's hospital in Unthank Road – now called the Colman Hospital] to consider arrangements for treating air-raid casualties. The committee appointed by the Board of Management to go into the matter reported on 31st December 1935 that they did not consider the city a suitable place for a base hospital owing to its being an obvious military target. They advised in the event of war the Jenny Lind should be asked to take charge of the children in the Norfolk and Norwich and that one hundred beds in the hospital should be retained as a casualty clearing station. If the suggestion that a base hospital should be established in the vicinity of Norwich were adopted, they considered that the Norfolk and Norwich could provide the specialist medical and nursing staff necessary for a hospital of from two hundred to three hundred beds. They asked for instructions in anti-gas measures and the first-aid treatment of air-raid casualties."

On Thursday 9th July 1936 a Home Office official advised on the formation, consisting of male hospital staff, of "fire and decontamination squads, and that the architect should prepare plans for making the basements proof against gas and blast.

"On 2nd September 1936 the Hospital's Air Raid Precautions Committee submitted a report on hospital services in the event of war. They advised that the Norfolk County Council be asked to select four or five Public Assistance Institutions - the modern name for the old workhouse – in different parts of the county which could each furnish a hundred or a hundred and fifty beds staffed by local doctors and volunteer nurses, for use in emergency."

The Norfolk and Norwich Hospital organized a mobile unit with "four members of the honorary medical staff, two resident medical officers, and twenty-four nursing staff which would be ready to go where needed to deal with all urgent and serious casualties."

In March 1937 the county authorities agreed to the Institution idea, and offered Aylsham, Gressenhall, Pulham Market and Thetford. "Each was asked to be prepared to set aside beds for casualties which the hospital's mobile unit would visit as suggested. The Institution at Lingwood, which members of the Board and staff of the hospital had inspected, could be adapted for the reception of one hundred cases from the hospital."

The Norfolk and Norwich Hospital began getting ready as the situation deteriorated. "By 1938 the Government had realized that the danger was great and imminent and could only be met by mobilization of all hospital services and by preparations for defence on a far more extensive scale than those so far somewhat tentatively suggested."

In May 1938 "the Medical Officer of Health asked for the out-patient department to be converted into a First Aid Post" and later in September "The Matron asked the chairman of the Board for instructions on the steps to be taken for safeguarding the patients and nursing and domestic staff in the event of an air attack. Everyone expected that enemy planes would be over this country as soon as war was declared."

Arthur Cleveland stated that "The value of the work done by the A.R.P. [Air Raid Precautions] Committee in 1936 and 1937 now became apparent." He goes on to record that "In January 1939 the staff recommended the organization of a blood transfusion unit, as they rightly anticipated that this remedy would be in great demand in the treatment of serious injuries."

In the Norfolk and Norwich Hospital's Annual Report for 1939, signed off by 'A. J. Cleveland', dealing with the last four months of the year he stated that "The hospital is playing its part in the National Service. It is ready with accommodation for the admission of patients suffering from injuries as the result of an air-raid should the need arise and its out-patient and Casualty Departments have been adapted and equipped as a First Aid Post. The Board confidently trusts that the public of Norfolk and Norwich will provide the necessary means to maintain its fullest efficiency, the need for which was never greater than in these difficult times, when no-one can say to what service the Hospital will be called upon to render."

Sunday 3rd September 1939. "The first night of the war was one which none of us is likely to forget. We heard that London had had a false alarm in the morning, but it was not until we were awakened by the wailing cry, whose very note is sinister, that we realized that we were directly faced with a danger all the more unnerving because it was unknown and came in the dark."

The Town Clerk of Norwich, Bernard Storey wrote "The warning of the eleven sirens in the city was a false alarm, but it began a series of 1,443 alerts, an average of one a day for the next four years. By no means all heralded a real attack – some few of them came too late unfortunately to do so – but these few unheralded incidents led high quarters to yield to the City Council's urgent representations in March 1941 to authorize a public 'crash warning' system of imminent danger between the hours of 6am and 11am."

Arthur Cleveland wrote that "When war began the air-raid shelters in Norwich could only accommodate 17,000 persons – a seventh of the population – and it was not until the beginning of 1942 that there were sufficient for all."

City of Norwich.

MEMBERS OF PARLIAMENT.

Sir Geoffrey H. Shakespeare, Bart., 69, Westminster Gardens, Whitehall, S.W.1.
H. G. Strauss, Esq., 25, Cheyne Walk, S.W.3.

MEMBERS OF THE COUNCIL, 1942-43.

Lord Mayor—Arthur J. Cleveland, Esq., O.B.E., M.D., F.R.C.P., 34, Cathedral Close, Norwich.
Sheriff—Councillor J. Brooksbank, J.P., 8, Suckling Avenue, Mile Cross, Norwich.
Deputy Lord Mayor—Alderman F. C. Jex, J.P., Natuna, Catton Grove Road, Norwich.

ALDERMEN.

J. H. Barnes, J.P., 160, Angel Road.
B. Cannell, 73 and 75, Barrack Street.
M. M. Clarkson (Miss), C.B.E., J.P., 5, Mount Pleasant.
H. Deacon, 2, Matlock Road.
G. H. Finn, 433, Unthank Road.
H. Frazer, J.P., 19, Elm Grove Lane.
F. J. Henderson, J.P., 419, Earlham Road.
M. High (Mrs.), 73, Bishopgate.
W. Hindes, J.P., 9, Tillett Road.
G. F. Johnson, 16, Pelham Road.
W. A. Riley, J.P., 5, St. Alban's Road.
H. C. Southgate, Sherwood, Cotman Road.
W. E. Walker, J.P., 35, Trory Street.
C. Watling, J.P., 43, All Saints' Green.
H. E. Witard, J.P., Brookend, Brooke.

COUNCILLORS.

H. Allen, 78, Harvey Lane.
G. H. Amond, 24, Rye Avenue.
S. A. Bailey, 9, Grove Road.
A. E. Baines, 447, Unthank Road.
E. S. Blake, 104, College Road.
P. J. Boddy, 8, Hughenden Road.
J. Owen Bond, 499, Unthank Road.
R. P. Braund, 20, All Saints Green. (Private : Weston, Constitution Hill.)
F. C. Browne, J.P., 59, Woodcock Road.
Michael Bulman, M.D., M.S., 101, Newmarket Road.
F. E. Burdett (Mrs.), J.P., 17, Corie Road.
J. S. Bush, The Retreat, Horstead, Nr. Coltishall.
O. H. Carter, 211, Newmarket Road.
G. J. Carver, 83, Elizabeth Fry Road.
W. Channell, Keir Hardie Hall, St. Gregory's Alley.
B. H. Clarke, 60, Wolfe Road.
J. F. Coales, 1a, Blickling Court, Recorder Road.
J. J. Cornwell, 113, Mile Cross Road.
W. G. Cutbush, J.P., 4, Spynke Road, Mile Cross.
P. V. Daley, 12, Rye Avenue.

The Norwich Annual *for 1943 published detailed information concerning the running of the City of Norwich. This page was followed by a list of Councillors (47); Justices of the Peace (32); Committees (15); and 20 Municipal Officers not including 'Elective Auditors'.*

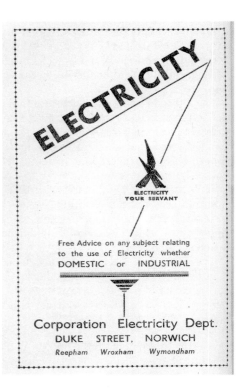

The Lord Mayor's position was that of Chairman of Norwich City Council during his year of office. The city, with a population of something like 113,000 was administered by 15 Aldermen and 47 Councillors. There were 32 Justices of the Peace, and a number of committees such as the Museums Committee, City Committee, Education Committee, Electricity Committee [the city had its own electricity department in Duke Street], Executive Committee, Finance Committee, Health Committee, Housing Committee, Markets Committee, Parks Committee, Libraries Committee, Watch Committee and Water Committee. There was also the Norwich Assessment Committee and the Social Welfare Committee. There were 8 District Medical Officers; Woodlands Hospital in Bowthorpe Road, and the Children's Homes of which there were 29 'Receiving Homes', and 80 'Scattered Homes'. Of these the regulations were strict. 'Parents and near relatives have permission to visit the children on the first Sunday in each month, and at other times under conditions approved by the Children's Committee, by previously obtaining a visitors card from the Superintendent of Chairman. It is unnecessary to bring or send parcels containing food. All parcels brought to the children must be handed to the Officer of the Home. No child, without special permission, will be permitted to leave the home with relatives. Any infringement of the rules, or interference with the committee's control of the children, may result in the permission to visit being withdrawn' said the *Norwich Annual* for 1943, though compiled in December 1942.

Public parks and the like also had to be looked after. There was Castle Gardens (3 acres), Cathedral Gardens in the Upper and Lower Close, Chapel Field Gardens (8½ acres), Eagle Baths in Heigham Street, Earlham Park (160 acres), Eaton Park (80 acres), Gildencroft Recreation Ground in St Augustine's (2 acres), Heigham Park in Recreation Road (6 acres),

Hellesdon Hill Meadow in Low Road Hellesdon, Hellesdon Recreation Ground (29 acres), Jenny Lind Playground in Pottergate, Jubilee Playground at Lakenham (8 acres), Kett's Cave in Morley Street and Mousehold Street (3½ acres), King Street Playground, Lakenham Baths in Martineau Lane, Lakenham Recreation Ground in City Road (1½ acres), Mile Cross Gardens in Aylsham Road (1½ acres), Mousehold Heath (190 acres), Mousehold Woodland Estate (31 acres), Municipal Golf Course off Bluebell Road (118 acres), Priory Playground in Cowgate, St. James Hollow in Gurney Road Mousehold (6 acres), Sewell Park off Constitution Hill (3 acres), The James Stuart Gardens by Recorder Road (½ acre), Waterloo Park in Angel Road (17 acres), Wensum Park off Drayton Road (8 acres), Wensum View Recreation Ground by Dereham Road (1 acre), Woodlands Plantation off Dereham Road (6½ acres) and Woodrow Pilling Park in Harvey Lane, Thorpe (7½ acres).

Besides the committees, the City Hall also housed the office of Registration of Births, Deaths, and Marriages. There was the Norwich Cemetery off the Earlham Road to look after, the Rosary Cemetery in Rosary Road, and the Norwich and Norfolk Crematorium off the Cromer Road at Horsham St. Faiths. In the Norwich Cemetery "For the exclusive right of burial in perpetuity, a grave 8 feet by 4 feet £3.10.0. For the right to construct a vault or walled grave with the exclusive right of burial therein in perpetuity 6 feet by 4 feet £4.10.0".

At the Rosary a single grave ground purchase price was £5, or a double grave £10. Internment cost £2.10.0. At the Crematorium 'For a Cremation including the use of the Chapel, Waiting-rooms and portable organ, and all attendances after the body is placed on the Catafalque by Undertakers - £6.6.0. Children under 6 years of age - £3.3.0. Children under 12 years of age - £5.5.0. For use of organ and services of an organist - £1.1.0. For decorating the Chapel with plants and flowers – from £2.2.0. For caskets to contain the Ashes – from £1.5.0'.

In wartime Norwich at this time the ARP were much in evidence with First Aid Posts and Cleansing Stations at Colman Road School, at the Sussex Street ARP Headquarters, at Stuart School in Telegraph Lane, and at the Norfolk and Norwich Hospital. There were Cleansing Stations only at Angel Road School near Waterloo Park, Duke Street School, and Lakenham School in City Road.

There were Emergency Feeding Centres in Angel Road Senior Girls School, Bull Close Infants School, Blyth Secondary School by Constitution Hill, Anguish's Housecraft School in Hall Road, Cavell Primary School in Duckett Close, Alderman Jex Senior Boys School in Sprowston Road, Dowson Senior Girls School in Valpy Avenue, Heigham House School in West Pottergate, Catton Grove Primary School in Peterson Road, Larkman Lane Senior School in Clarkson Road, Wensum View Senior School in Waterworks Road, Willow Lane Primary School and Colman Road Open Air School by South Park Avenue.

There were also Rest Centres and a couple of British Restaurants where reasonably priced wholesome meals could be had at Bull Close School and Duke Street School.

The Lower Cathedral Close fire watching team consisting of, left to right, Arthur Cleveland who lived at No. 34 The Close, the silversmith Howard Brown standing and his wife in front who lived at No. 50, Evelyn Cleveland and their daughter Deenie Cleveland at the back, and, it is believed, the poet and painter Camilla Doyle of No. 46 in the front next to the stirrup pump. Dr. Cleveland had a brick and concrete air raid shelter built in the back garden of No. 34. The shelter was big enough for several people, and other locals were invited in if the necessity arose. There were public air raid shelters across the city, one being not far from The Close - No. 4 which had painted on it 'ARP Public Shelter. Capacity 50 persons'.

At Air Raid Wardens' Posts volunteers watched for enemy action and resulting fires. There were 75 such posts across Norwich. Because of the danger of fires the city was covered with Auxiliary Fire Stations at Bethel Street, Chapel Field Road, Sayer Street, Surrey Street, Prince of Wales Road, Barrack Street, Silver Road and Mousehold Lane.

Instructions given were "In the event of an air raid send a message to the nearest Fire Station in preference to telephoning". Another said "In the event of extensive damage by air raids, an office will be opened at the City Hall where questions arising as a result of the raid will be dealt with, such as Billeting [finding a place to stay], Furniture Removal and Storage, Food Cards, Compensation for Damage, Replacement of Clothing, Financial Help etc." So Norwich was organised in wartime.

As for enemy action, not a lot happened in Norwich after war was declared. The nearest incident was off the Norfolk coast during January 1940 when a Trinity House lightship service vessel was attacked killing one person and injuring others, and the East Dudgeon lightship was bombed on

Monday 29th January with seven of the crew of eight dying when their rowing life-boat capsized.

The first high explosive bomb to fall on Norfolk soil fell harmlessly in a field at Raynham, near Fakenham on Friday 24th May. Although Norwich had prepared itself as we have seen, no bombs fell on the city for the time being.

The first air raid on Norwich occurred during the afternoon of Tuesday 9th July 1940 when bombs fell on Barnard's wire netting factory in Salhouse Road, Mousehold, and the Carrow Hill and King Street areas including Boulton and Paul's works on Riverside Road where 10 workers were killed and 68 injured. Some damage also occurred to the railway lines behind Thorpe Station. In all 27 people were killed. No one died during the next raid early in the morning of Friday 19th of July when bombs fell in the Botolph Street and Magdalen Street area of the city, but 11 were killed during an early morning raid on Tuesday 30th July when much damage was done in Surrey Street including the bus station in Ber Street, and Colman's Works by the River Wensum.

Clearing up in Botolph Street after the raid on Norwich on Friday 19th of July 1940. This photograph, and many that follow, was taken by Norwich photographer George Swain.

King Street, Boulton and Paul's joinery works, and Thorpe Railway Station [now Norwich Station] received hits during the afternoon of Thursday 1st August resulting in over a dozen deaths – nine of whom worked at Boulton and Paul's Riverside works. No one died and very little damage was done when there was a raid on Saturday 10th August when three bombs were dropped, one of which hit Colman's Carrow works. The next raid was in the early hours of Tuesday 20th August when incendiary bombs landed in the city with the fires quickly put out by air raid wardens, and an unexploded bomb in Theatre Street had to be dealt with. There were no casualties.

There was a big fire in the Back of The Inns area on Wednesday 23rd October, but this was nothing to do with enemy action - just a blaze which originated in the Busmen's Social Club above Craske's butchers shop, which destroyed the stationers and printing works of Henry T. King and the Haymarket public house in White Lion Street.

No-one died during a raid on Sunday 27th October, nor during the one on 1st November when a few bombs were dropped in the Larkman Road area. Incendiary bombs caused fires in Thorpe on 11th November but no one was hurt. However five people were killed during the raid on the Monday evening of 2nd December when a bomb caused much damage next to Willmott's shop in Prince of Wales Road; a house was demolished in Bracondale; another in St. John Street; and the Orchard Tavern in Mountergate Street was badly damaged. A girl of 18 died when a house was hit at Carrow Hill on Wednesday 11th December.

Joan Banger, in her *Norwich at War,* lists on Monday 16th December an "unfortunate incident occurred when one of our own planes dropped bombs in the Dereham Road area. One fell on Howes Garage in Bond Street." There were no casualties.

The last raid of 1940 on Norwich was on Saturday 21st December in the Mile Cross area. No one was hurt.

The remains of The Orchard Tavern in Mountergate Street after the raid of Monday 2nd December 1940.

George Swain took many photographs following air raids during the war, this one showing the extent of the damage in Vauxhall Street after the raid on 18th February 1941.

1941 began with an air raid on Sunday January 5th with no casualties, though a month later, on 4th February, two people died after houses were damaged in the Plumstead Road area and the works of Boulton and Paul's was hit again. Eight people died during the raid on Tuesday 18th February when a large bomb exploded in Vauxhall Street. Barnard's factory on the Salhouse Road again suffered damage on 27th February; luckily there were no casualties, and nor were there any during the raids of 14th March and 30th March.

On Wednesday 2nd April an employee of Steward and Patteson's brewery [Pockthorpe Brewery in Barrack Street] was killed during an early afternoon raid, and one person died following the raid of 29th April. Three people died of injuries after a late night raid of the 5th of May, and a couple of days later on Wednesday 7th May three children and their parents died during a raid at 10 o'clock at night in Cadge Road - between Dereham Road and Earlham Road.

Raids on Norwich continued on 10th May, 17th May, 30th July, and 8th August of that year of 1941. No one was killed but the sirens, circling aircraft, explosions and fires must have been very frightening and unsettling. Then there were the rescue operations, seeing to casualties, finding homes for the bombed out, and generally clearing up the mess which must have added to the anxiety of war. However, there were no more raids for the next eight months.

Protecting glass and shutters up for the blackout on George Swain's photographic shop and business at 27 St. Giles, almost next door to the Hippodrome Theatre- which was roughly opposite the City Hall car park.

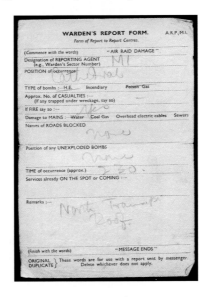

Air raid warden Laurence Malster's report after seeing an incendiary bomb set fire to the North Transept of Norwich Cathedral at 2.30am on Saturday 27th June 1942. Mr. Malster quickly filled in this form, then "replaced it by one more legibly written." M1 refers to the local A.R.P. Post on Tombland.

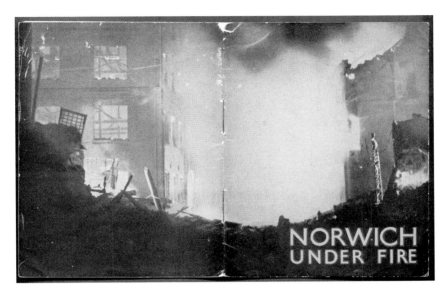

The cover of George Swain's booklet Norwich Under Fire, *here opened up to reveal the whole picture of 'The fire in Westwick Street on 27th April, 1942.' George Swain used a bicycle to get round Norwich to take photographs at this time. His photography shop was his base where all the developing and printing was carried out. It was at No. 27 St. Giles, next to the old Hippodrome Theatre – now the site of an underground car park. Upstairs in the shop was the photographic studio complete with dressing rooms where George and his sister Muriel Noller took people's studio portraits.*

1942

1942 began quietly for the City of Norwich, with very little happening. It all changed on Monday 27th April. Edward Le Grice, grocer and photographer of Merton Road [between Dereham Road and Bowthorpe Road] wrote in his *Norwich – The Ordeal of 1942*, "A lovely night. The old city bathed in moonlight. Suddenly the silence was broken by the wail of sirens, the distant throb of engines, the menacing roar of aircraft growing louder, and the night sky was illuminated with the red glare from floating chandeliers of coloured lights like giant fireworks hovering over the city. Then all hell was let loose over a defenceless people, and Norwich was facing the ordeal of 1942."

This was a substantial two hour attack on the city with over fifty tons of bombs dropped resulting in 162 people being killed, some 600 hundred casualties, and much damage. Dr. Arthur Cleveland wrote "By the light of flares which showed every building as clearly as daylight 185 high explosive bombs and numerous incendiaries were dropped by some 25 to 30 planes. The raid developed so quickly that there were very few members of the male staff at the hospital when we started to move the patients from the top floors to the basements, but the sisters, nurses, and resident medical officers with other help soon got the top wards clear. At the same time the hot water, steam and gas were turned off in the basement and eventually the patients were all got to the basement. Before the 'All Clear' signal was given, air-raid casualties started to arrive and that night we admitted 87 patients and dealt with 95 out-patient casualties. Considerable damage by blast had been done to various parts of the hospital."

George Swain, photographer, recorded in his *Norwich Under Fire* booklet "My busiest night of picture-making was the night of 27 April 1942. Everybody who went through it remembers just where he was and what he did that Monday night. I was at Thorpe when the siren sounded at 11 o'clock, and I set out on my bicycle for the centre of the city, where smoke and flames were rising. Flares were hanging in the sky and red tracer bullets were making spurts and lines of fire everywhere. Bombs were whistling down. One particularly close, threw me from my bicycle – or perhaps I threw myself off - and I dived through a garden gate. A few minutes later, in Westwick Street, I was taking some of the fire pictures you will find in this book."

On Tuesday clearing up began. At the Norfolk and Norwich Hospital forty workmen from Yarmouth and twelve from the Norwich building firm of J. Youngs & Son, began repairing the damaged roofs and making the wards weatherproof. All over the city people were busy.

The fire blitz on Norwich began on Monday 27th April 1942
at 11.30 at night. This is Bonds store on All Saint's Green
burning - from George Swain's book Norwich Under Fire.

Rampant Horse Street looking up towards Theatre Street. The premises on the left were then Buntings the drapers, and further along Woolworths.

Wrecked properties in Westwick Street.

Lothian Street, off Barn Road.

George Swain wrote in his Norwich Under Fire *'St Benedict's ancient church is severely damaged - 27-29th April 1942'.*

Damage to the 2000 seat Odeon cinema in Botolph Street. The cinema opened in 1938.

St. Benedict's Street. Note the cat on the left in this George Swain picture from his Norwich Under Fire.

That Tuesday night - the 28th - there was an 'alert' but nothing came of it. However on Wednesday 29th April there was another severe attack on the city, with "Forty-five tons of heavy bombs and many incendiaries dropped. Sixty-nine people killed, 89 seriously injured" recorded Harold Jaffa in his *Norfolk Events* compiled from the *Eastern Daily Press* in 1950. At the hospital casualties began to arrive, but after twenty-five had been admitted they had to stop as fire was raging in St. Stephens and the ambulances could not get through. They were diverted to Woodlands Hospital [now known as the Norwich Community Hospital] in Bowthorpe Road. At the Norfolk and Norwich they were hampered when "the electricity failed for half an hour. The external telephone also failed and we utilized the emergency battery set for the internal telephones. This failed after half an hour, but eventually we got it working. The outside telephone was not working for several hours and we had to send messengers to the Report Centre" wrote Dr. Cleveland.

Many families suffered in the raid, but for the Burton family it was tragic when their home at 46 Alexandra Road [between Earlham Road and Dereham Road] was hit. Four were killed - Ernest John Burton, a bricklayer aged 56 died along with his wife Clara Burton aged 53, and their son John Ernest Frank Burton, a grocer's assistant aged 18, and their daughter Sybil Constance, aged 13. Steve Snelling in his *Norwich - a Shattered City*, said "Four members of the Burton family were the victims. The irony was that Ernest Burton was employed building brick air-raid shelters for the corporation but refused to have his own Anderson shelter." The sight of the temporary crosses on the row of graves in Norwich Cemetery was a chilling reminder of the devastation of war.

These two 'blitz' attacks were designed to destroy as much as possible, and became known as Baedeker Raids after the guide book maps of this German company showed Norwich as an historic city. Much damage was done to buildings and people's houses. Those two days of death and destruction had repercussions for the people and fabric of the city for years to come.

A further raid took place in the early hours of Friday 1st May when, amongst other buildings affected, Harmer's clothing factory in St Andrews Street [opposite the end of Exchange Street] was set on fire. On Saturday 9th

Repairs begin. The April 1942 raids on Norwich were the most severe of the war.

of May bombs fell in the early hours on Woodlands Hospital in Bowthorpe Road doing much damage but no one was hurt.

It remained quiet until the raid in the early hours of Saturday 27th June when nine people died. Many incendiary bombs were dropped on the city that night resulting in fires in St Stephens, All Saints Green and Timber Hill. The Cathedral roof was set alight. At the Norfolk and Norwich Hospital 120 beds were put out of commission and eighty nurses and maids made homeless when the roof of the Leicester Nurses Home was set ablaze,

At the hospital the roofs of Wards 3 & 4 were completely burnt and Wards 1 & 2 beneath were damaged during the raid of Saturday 27th June.

and the second and third floors were badly damaged. Dr. Cleveland recorded that the 'fire blitz' as he called it, had severely damaged the hospital. "Many nurses and maids lost everything but the clothes they had on. The main operating theatres and the linen room over them were destroyed and with the latter a large and valuable store of linen. That the damage done was not much worse was due in no small measure to the promptness and pluck displayed by the fire fighters.

The Leicester Nurses Home roof was set ablaze and the second and third floors badly damaged. The Home had been opened in 1903.

"Our first task was the removal of all patients from the threatened buildings, and in this we were assisted by many neighbours and members of the city's defence organisation. Soldiers stationed near the hospital lent a willing hand, and when the raid was over and we looked on the ruin it had caused we could at least be thankful that no one had been hurt. In the early hours of the morning the hospital grounds presented a curious sight. All around on the lawns and paths were patients on mattresses among chairs, tables, office records, surgical instruments, nurses' clothes, and everything that could be moved out of danger. To be in the centre of a city which is being heavily bombed is an unpleasant and frightening experience for anyone."

Five people died when a "new type of explosive incendiary" was dropped on the city on the Sunday 2nd August, and on Monday 19th October Duke Street [between Charing Cross and Colegate] and Westwick Street [between Charing Cross and Barn Road] were bombed and the Jenny Lind Hospital was hit as well.

The Lord Mayor at this time was John Henry Barnes, who had shown King George VI around the city during a surprise visit on Tuesday 12th October 1942 to see how Norwich had coped with the air raids. The King looked at the damage, visited the Norfolk and Norwich Hospital in St. Stephens Road and toured a factory. The Press said "Girl factory workers in Norwich looked up from their machines to find the King standing beside them. 'If I had known we were to have a Royal visit I would have cleaned myself up' remarked one of the girls."

Dr. Cleveland, who showed the King round the Hospital accompanied by the Lord Mayor, described the visit of the King in his book *A History of the Norfolk and Norwich Hospital*, as 'unofficial', and that "The absence of ceremony and the gracious and sympathetic manner in which he chatted to us and inspected our damaged buildings served as a tonic to patients and staff alike."

The mayoral year for John Barnes and the Sheriff Clifford White was drawing to a close.

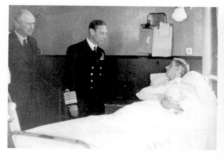 

The King at the Norfolk and Norwich Hospital with Dr. Cleveland during his 'unofficial' visit to the city on Tuesday 12th October 1942.

The new Lord Mayor of Norwich, Dr. A. J. Cleveland, outside the City Hall after the Mayor Making ceremony in the Council Chamber on Monday 9th November 1942. From the left, after the two officials, there is Mrs. Brooksbank; The Under Sheriff Percy Hatch at the back; the Sheriff John Brooksbank; the Town Clerk Bernard Storey behind; the Lord Mayor; the Chief Constable of Norwich City Police John Henry Dain behind; the Lady Mayoress Evelyn Cleveland, and on the right the Deputy Lord Mayor Alderman F. C. Jex. At the back right two officials.

The New Lord Mayor's Year Begins

In Norwich on Monday 9th November 1942 Dr. Arthur John Cleveland was "unanimously elected and installed as Lord Mayor and John Brooksbank as Sheriff" reported the *Eastern Daily Press*.

Norwich did occasionally appoint a Lord Mayor (the 'Lord' prefix was added in February 1910 giving the office a more prestigious name - it did not come with a seat in the House of Lords!) outside the Council members which "enabled a fresh outlook and a different point of view to be brought to its deliberations, and showed that every man and woman in the city had an opportunity to hold the chief position in local government" said Mr. W. A. Riley of the Conservative Party.

Alderman Riley had proposed Dr. Cleveland in September as the next Lord Mayor. "He had never engaged himself in political affairs" said Mr. Riley, "but his name was known far outside the confines of this city, notably as chairman of the Norfolk and Norwich Hospital." This was the fourth time in the previous seventy years that a medical man became what Mr. Riley called the "chief citizen of Norwich."

The writer of the 'Whiffler' column in the *Eastern Evening News* witnessed the proceedings on that Monday. "Precisely at 11 o'clock the doors of the Council Chamber were flung open to the cry 'His Worship the Lord Mayor'. Aldermen, Councillors and visitors rose to their feet. A small but dignified procession entered the Chamber. First the Lord Mayor's officer in ceremonial dress; secondly the Town Clerk [Bernard Storey] in wig and gown; thirdly the Lord Mayor [John Barnes] in splendid apparel; fourthly the Sheriff [Clifford White] in more sober robes; and finally the Deputy Lord Mayor in brighter gown. It was a full dress parade - the last entry of J. H. Barnes as Lord Mayor 1941-2. Alderman Riley proposed the new Lord Mayor Dr. A. J. Cleveland. The Council, having unanimously elected Dr. Cleveland Lord Mayor for the ensuing year, another procession entered the chamber. This time the tall figure of Dr. Cleveland, robed, was the centre of it. Everyone stood up and remained on his feet whilst Dr. Cleveland swore, Bible in hand, the customary oaths. Alderman Barnes then took off his chain of office and the new Lord Mayor, donning it, took his seat as chief citizen."

So it was on Monday 9th November 1942 that Arthur John Cleveland began his mayoral year. "He expressed a feeling of pride and humility and a determination to do his utmost to further the welfare and prosperity of the city" reported the *Eastern Daily Press* the next day. He also announced that he had appointed Alderman F. C. Jex as his deputy.

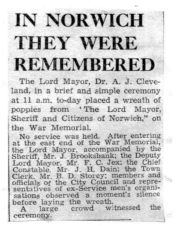

IN NORWICH THEY WERE REMEMBERED

The Lord Mayor, Dr. A. J. Cleveland, in a brief and simple ceremony at 11 a.m. to-day placed a wreath of poppies from 'The Lord Mayor, Sheriff and Citizens of Norwich," on the War Memorial.

No service was held. After entering at the east end of the War Memorial, the Lord Mayor, accompanied by the Sheriff, Mr. J. Brooksbank; the Deputy Lord Mayor, Mr. F. C. Jex; the Chief Constable, Mr. J. H. Dain; the Town Clerk, Mr. B. D. Storey; members and officials of the City Council and representatives of ex-Service men's organisations observed a moment's silence before laying the wreath.

A large crowd witnessed the ceremony.

The Eastern Evening News *of Wednesday 11th November 1942 reported that in the morning the Lord Mayor had laid a wreath of poppies on the Norwich War Memorial.*

The first undertaking for the new Lord Mayor was on Armistice Day, Wednesday the 11th November at 11am, when a large crowd watched as he laid a wreath of poppies from 'The Lord Mayor, Sheriff and Citizens of Norwich' on the War Memorial in front of the City Hall. He was accompanied by the Sheriff - John Brooksbank; the Deputy Lord Mayor - Alderman Jex; the Chief Constable of Norwich City Police - John Dain; the Town Clerk - Bernard Storey, and representatives from ex-service men's organisations. "There has been a generous response from the Norwich public to the sale of poppies in the city and Mrs. Palmer, the organiser, stated last evening that they had every hope of reaching their aim of £1300" reported the *Eastern Daily Press* the next day.

The next appointment for Arthur Cleveland was when he "presided at his first public meeting during his year of office" as the local paper put it, of the Association of Friends of the French Volunteers and the Norwich French Circle at the Stuart Hall [now part of the Cinema City complex] in St. Andrews Street on Saturday 14th November.

Mademoiselle Yvonne Salmon, honorary secretary of the Alliance Francaise, gave "a witty and well-informed speech on The Fighting French. Mademoiselle Salmon described how General De Gaulle arrived in this country at the moment of France's collapse and started the Free French Movement to organise resistance with the object of assisting the Allied Nations in restoring France and paving the way to victory over the aggressor."

After her talk she was "thanked on behalf of the meeting by Mr. R. H. Mottram [a Justice of the Peace and well known author] and the Lord Mayor. Dr. Howes remarked that this civic honour accorded to the cause of Free France would be of the greatest service. In reply, the Lord Mayor alluded to the great debt which civilisation owed to French science, art and literature, and said how essential it was that she should be restored to her proper place in the world." The Lord Mayor accepted the position of honorary president of the local association, and "Tea was served from Curate's House [restaurant in the Haymarket], the proprietor, Mr. Levy, kindly handing over the proceeds to the funds of the local association."

That Saturday morning there appeared in the *Eastern Daily Press* a letter, written by the Lord Mayor the day before, concerning his feelings for the American forces men who were now arriving in this country. Following a meeting of the American Red Cross and the Ministry of Information about welcoming Americans, Dr. Cleveland wrote about providing "hospitality and entertainment for our American visitors" as he put it. "It is felt that the best form of initial approach would be through dances, sports, concerts and similar events offered and arranged by local organisations, whose members could make acquaintance at such functions with our American friends. These 'getting to know each other' gatherings would, it is hoped, result in personal offers of private hospitality." This initiative to which the Lord Mayor gave his "hearty approval" resulted in many people, including Arthur Cleveland and his wife, making life-long American friends.

Hospitality to Americans

Sir—There are, I am sure, many citizens and organisations anxious to offer hospitality in one form or another to the Americans, but how to effect these good intentions presents difficulties.

At a meeting of representatives of Norwich and Norfolk, which was recently convened, an Executive Committee was appointed to consider, in collaboration with the Ministry of Information and the American Red Cross, the problem of providing hospitality and entertainment for our American visitors. Sub-committees for city and county are being formed.

It is felt that the best form of initial approach would be through dances, sports, concerts and similar events offered and arranged by local organisations, whose members could make acquaintance at such functions with our American friends. These " getting to know each other " gatherings would, it is hoped, result in personal offers of private hospitality.

This suggestion of hospitality through organisations has my hearty approval and I am. therefore, writing in the hope that the committees may receive such offers from organisations upon the lines indicated. This, of course, does not preclude offers of private hospitality. Letters should be addressed for the city to Mr. C. Graham Harbord, 19, Upper King-st., and for the county to Mr. W. H. H. Middleton, 12, The Close, marked "American Hospitality," and should specify the nature of the entertainment offered, the number of guests and the date, time and place suggested.—Yours faithfully,

ARTHUR J. CLEVELAND,
Lord Mayor.
Norwich, Nov. 13.

Arthur Cleveland's letter concerning American personnel now being based in the region published in the Eastern Daily Press *on Saturday14th November 1942, encouraging a 'getting to know each other' campaign.*

Sunday 15th November was 'Civic Sunday and Civil Defence Day', and the Lord Mayor and Lady Mayoress, the Sheriff and Deputy Lord Mayor, attended at 11 o'clock a service in the Cathedral. "Crowds watched Civil Defence, RAF and WAFF [Women's Auxiliary Air Force] personnel, numbering about 400, who, headed by the Lads Club Band, marched from the City Hall to the Cathedral, where they were joined by an Army contingent."

The occasion was accompanied by bells being rung in Norwich churches. "Although a shortage of bell-ringers had been feared, volunteers, including several members of the forces brought the number up to 19, making it possible to ring up the bells not only of St. Peter Mancroft and St. Giles, but also St. Michael at Coslany. The Cathedral bells were chimed, and those of most other parish churches in the city were sounded. The bell of St. Anne's, Earlham, which was saved when the church was burnt out in one of the Norwich raids of early summer, was rung again from a temporary stage close to the ruined church" said a report on the proceedings. The sermon was preached by the Dean and the collection was in aid of Norfolk and Norwich Medical Charities.

Wednesday 18th November was a busy day for the Lord Mayor. He took up his position as senior magistrate at the City Police Court. He was welcomed by the officials of the Bench who hoped his year of office would be a happy one. He replied that he had been in a court before when "As a young boy I was hauled up before the magistrates for poaching, and in recent years I was before the magistrates for leaving my motor car unattended."

His next appointment that day was at the Norwich Rotary Club lunch where he gave a speech which allowed him to say something about conditions in the latter part of the 19th century when he was a student at Guy's Hospital in London. He began by saying that we must not judge earlier generations by today's standards, but by those of their own time. "Employers of those days were humane, devout men who firmly believed that the law of supply and demand would regulate and right economic inequalities. The poor themselves did not wish for any change in the system because they were afraid it would increase the price of food. To suggest that anything was wrong with the country's economic system would have been regarded as heresy. It was a curious paradox that the very development that produced these slums produced also the cure. Most of the advantages we enjoy today were the result of inventions of last century.

"Two factors which had contributed much to the higher standard of hygiene among women were the fashions of short hair and short skirts. I regret to see the growing habit among girls of wearing their hair not only long but permanently waved, so that in many cases it does not get as much brushing and combing as it ought to do.

"Better wages, Army training and the influence of hospitals were other factors which had helped to bring about a better standard of hygiene. People had realised that personal hygiene added materially to their health and happiness."

The next day, Thursday 19th November, he presented to the City's Special Constabulary 111 long service medal ribbons to officers and constables, and 17 certificates to others recording the award of long service bars. Normally nine years had to be served for special constables to qualify for the long service medal, and bars were presented for each additional ten years. In war conditions one year counted as three. In a speech he said "In this country we had such an excellent police service for so many years that we were apt not to appreciate its full value, and the citizens, probably, had not fully realised the tremendous burden the 'specials' had taken on their shoulders." Special Constables were civilians recruited locally as a back-up to the regular police force.

The Lady Mayoress, Evelyn Cleveland, had her duties to attend to as well. On Friday 27th November she presided over a meeting of the Norwich Branch of the National Council of Women at Suckling House [now part of the Cinema City complex], where the debate was about marriage by proxy. Mary Willis [a Justice of The Peace] said that "any alteration of marriage laws was a matter needing more serious consideration than the annual meeting could give. They had to remember they needed to protect men absent from the country as well as girls who might have reason to wish to marry." According to the report "Members expressed the view that the step was not always desirable in cases where a girl at home might wish to marry a soldier abroad, and the opinion was put forward that some alteration of pension laws, to provide for children of unmarried mothers whose fathers died on service abroad, would help partly to solve some of the problems marriage by proxy might be intended to meet." Evelyn Cleveland was also much interested in the work of the Y.W.C.A. [Young Women's Christian Association] and the hostel in Surrey Street, which she also threw her energies into.

Petrol was restricted but this did not stop the Norwich Motor Company advertising their vehicles and services. Their petrol station was on the corner of Recorder Road and Prince of Wales Road.

On the Sunday 29th November the Lord Mayor visited Nos. 231 and 233 Squadrons of the A.T.C. [Air Training Corps], watching open air activities and classroom teaching where the Cadets were learning various subjects including calculations and flight mechanics. The Wing Commander, Flt. Lt. A. A. Rice, explained that "in future the A.T.C. would open its doors to train those young men between the ages of fifteen years and three months and eighteen years who wanted to qualify as Army glider pilots. They would receive precisely the same training as those destined for the RAF. The ATC was thus training candidates for all three services" the Wing Commander said.

The Lord Mayor, presiding over a meeting of Norwich City Council on Friday 1st December, remarked on the generosity of Mr. Percy Moore Turner, a London art dealer, who donated a John Crome water-colour of 'The Blacksmiths Shop, Hingham' to the Castle Museum collection. Also given was a Gold Torc discovered while harrowing a field at Bawsey, near King's Lynn. The Council heard that this torc was "about 40 per cent. pure gold. It measures 8 inches in diameter and could only have been worn by a man of fine physique." Both the Crome water-colour and the gold torc were put on temporary view in the entrance hall of the Castle Museum.

Also at the meeting the Council passed a resolution of thanks to Mr. and Mrs. Russell Colman [Russell Colman was Lord Lieutenant of Norfolk] "For their public-spirited action in placing part of their residence at Crown Point at the disposal of the Council for the accommodation of patients from the Woodlands Hospital."

Miss M. Clarkson said she "felt that in this case the city's thanks were even more deserved for it was an acknowledgement of a gift of happiness and comfort to living people, most of whom, during long lives of hard work and poverty, and very often ill-health, in the main had had very little of such blessings. Some months ago Mr. and Mrs. Colman made the offer to accommodate at Crown Point 25 old and bedridden women who had been blitzed out of the Woodlands Hospital."

The Council agreed at that meeting to install a "wireless receiver, amplifier and wiring for 24 loud speaker points at a cost of £107 at St James Hospital, Shipmeadow [in Suffolk, between Beccles and Bungay], where other patients from Woodlands Hospital are being accommodated." Another resolution passed was for the building of three air raid shelters at the Great Hospital in Bishopgate costing £103.10.3d. Mr. W. A Riley said that "The Ministry would reimburse all but £15 of this."

Lady Baden-Powell, the Chief Guide, was in Norwich on Saturday 5th December. She said she last came to Norwich twenty-five years ago [1917] to see the beginning of the Guide movement in the city. Now she was in Norwich opening an exhibition and toy fair at the Y.W.C.A. The toys had been made by local people in the county and included such things, as Lady Baden-Powell said in her speech, "Dressed stuffed dolls, wooden toys, and woollen animals of every description showed how skill and ingenuity could make attractive things for children for the cost of only a few pence - in some cases without any cost. All the exhibits were made of old materials by individual Guiders or Guides and none had cost more than 6d to make."

The British Breakfast

A couple of pounds of beef steak and a pint of beer! Dinner before the war? No! Breakfast in the days of good Queen Bess. Even the bacon and eggs of pre-war breakfasts didn't equal that. As for the modern tea and toast....! But our ancestors knew a thing or two. Hard workers need *good* breakfasts. With longer hours, harder work, colder days, we've got to revive the substantial breakfast. Let *potatoes* swell the bacon ration, eke out the sausages, or double the size of a dried egg dish, all at the cost of a few pence. It needn't mean getting up any earlier if you will remember to cook extra potatoes the day before. Potatoes will give you the *extra* energy you need to carry on your war-time job, and help to keep you *fighting* fit.

RECIPE of the WEEK No. 23

POTATO PANCAKE

Ingredients: 1 lb. cooked potatoes, ¼ lb. sausage meat, 1 dessertspoonful mixed herbs and 1 dessertspoonful mint and parsley chopped together, salt, pepper, milk, ½ oz. dripping. **Quantity:** Four helpings. **Method:** Mash the potato with the sausage meat, add seasoning and milk to make a soft mixture. Heat dripping and spread potato mixture to cover the bottom of the pan. Fry till brown and crisp.

★ **Request of the Week**
Milk bottles are short, so be sure to return your empties to your roundsman every day.

THIS IS THE FIRST WEEK OF RATION PERIOD No. 3

SUGGESTIONS FOR BREAKFAST

SUNDAY: *Bacon and Fried Potatoes.*
MONDAY: *Irish Potato Omelet.*
TUESDAY: *Potato Cutlets.*
WEDNESDAY: *Potato Pancake.*
THURSDAY: *Potato Fadge and Bacon.*
FRIDAY: *Fish and Potato Pie.*
SATURDAY: *Potato Fritters and Sausages.*

POINTS REDUCTIONS
for the four weeks Sept. 20th — Oct. 17th

	POINTS
Home-produced meat roll from 4 to (in tins or slices)	2 per lb.
Eire stewed steak from 32 to	24
Grade 3 (Pink) salmon from 16 to	8
Broken biscuits (sold and described as such by the manufacturers)	Half the value of the whole biscuits in the same group—chocolate, sweet or plain

There will be no change in the value of Points coupons. The total number per person will remain at 20.

A = 1,   B = 2,   C = 2.

The personal ration remains at 1 lb. for the four-week period. Both coupon D and E counting 2 Points.

FOOD FACTS
NO. 116. THE MINISTRY OF FOOD, LONDON, W.1

Government information appeared in national and local newspapers and in short films shown in cinema programmes.

About £100 was raised which was invested in war savings. Unsold items were given to the Jenny Lind Hospital.

The Lord Mayor and Lady Mayoress attended a lunch given for the Chief Guide - who then went to the Drill Hall by Chapel Field Gardens where about 1000 Guides welcomed her, and she presented prizes to the winners of the Norfolk Guide toy competition. "She later left for the Y.W.C.A in a car drawn by 12 boy scouts" said a report of the day.

Wednesday 9th December. The Lord Mayor was at the Norwich headquarters of the Y.M.C.A. for their annual general meeting. In his speech he paid tribute to the organisation's work, saying "You are making good neighbours, and a good neighbour is not only a good citizen but is fulfilling the highest meaning of the name Christian." He went on to say "The mental welfare of the fighting soldier was as important as his physical welfare and that had been left to a great extent to organisations such as this. Almost all the great social movements in this country started as voluntary organisations and now, when we were coming to a stage in the development of our civilisation when some such voluntary bodies might have to be merged into government machinery, we ought not to lose sight of the great aims of educational movements such as the Y.M.C.A. If we could preserve some of the personal touch, the love of doing a good thing for its own sake, we should not lose so much as many were afraid we should when we reconstructed this country in accordance with the demands we should have to listen to."

The area secretary, Mr. G. F. Hubbard, reported on the work the Y.M.C.A. was doing for the men of the fighting services. This covered educational, cultural, religious and social activities, and the ambition to create a home-from-home atmosphere. Their work he said was growing steadily. He said the Y.M.C.A. stores department had handled 12,000,000 cigarettes, 600lbs of tobacco, 24 tons of chocolate, 30 tons of biscuits and 600 gross bars of soap. He gave details of mobile canteens and the part they played during the air raids on Norwich.

Dr. Cleveland, as Lord Mayor, was it seems in constant demand to attend functions and give speeches. One evening was a bit different, for he put on the event - a supper for the A.R.P. quiz team which had just won by 41 points to their opponents 34. He congratulated the team for winning, and after the meal thanked on behalf of the citizens of Norwich the Wardens "for the excellent work done by them in the City during the past three years. The Chief Warden, Victor Harrison, and the Sheriff, Mr. J. Brooksbank, thanked the Lord Mayor for his hospitality.

Dr. Cleveland composed and sent a message by telegram to King George VI on Monday 14th December expressing "loyal and sincere greetings on the occasion of His Majesty's Birthday." A reply came back thanking "my Lord Mayor and citizens of Norwich for your kind message of congratulations on my birthday. George R. I."

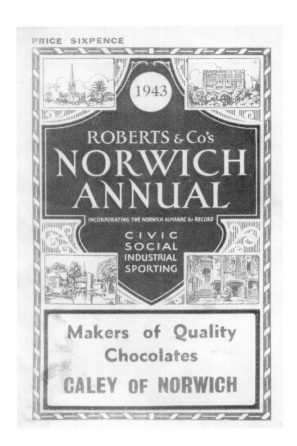

PRICE SIXPENCE

1943

ROBERTS & Co's
NORWICH
ANNUAL

INCORPORATING THE NORWICH ALMANAC & RECORD

CIVIC
SOCIAL
INDUSTRIAL
SPORTING

Makers of Quality
Chocolates

CALEY OF NORWICH

The Norwich Annual *for 1943 contained information on organisation and
running of the City of Norwich. This was published in December 1942.*

The Lord Mayor and Lady Mayoress attended a special Christmas
service of hymns and carols at Sun Lane Sunday School on 20th December
[Sun Lane - between Catton Grove Road and St Clements Hill]. The music
was provided by the band of the Norwich Lads Club and a collection was
taken for the Norwich Sunday School Union and the Jenny Lind Cot Fund.
The Mayor gave a speech recognising the important work carried out by the
school.

Sun Lane School was founded in 1818 following an initiative of the
Norwich Sunday School Union. At first a single room was hired in a cottage
in Long Row, Catton, but about 70 years later a new building was erected in
Sun Lane. It is said the school then had 900 children on its register. In 1908
the Methodist Church was built in Rosebery Road [between Catton Grove
Road and Magdalen Road] with which the school was connected.

On a more personal note, on Thursday 24th December Arthur Cleveland
became a grandfather, when the author of this book was born to John and
Mary Cleveland.

Christmas Day morning was a busy time for the Lord Mayor, Lady Mayoress, and the Sheriff and his wife, as they visited Norwich hospitals. At Woodlands Hospital they went round the surgical ward "where members of the Dereham Road Baptist and Belvoir Street Methodist choirs were entertaining the patients with carols." At the Norfolk and Norwich Hospital they toured one of the wards where "a house surgeon appeared armed with a carving knife. But it turned out that his patients were only six beautifully roasted chickens. Sausages, sprouts and mashed potatoes and glasses of beer completed the hospital Christmas dinner."

Great Hospital Charity, Bishopgate.

Founded by Walter de Suffield, Bishop of Norwich, about 1249, and originally known as St. Giles Hospital. Granted by Letters Patent in 1547 to the Corporation of Norwich by King Edward VI. and others under the will of King Henry VIII. Then called the "House of God or the House of the Poor in Holme Street." Since this date many benefactions have been made to this greatest of the ancient charitable institutions of Norwich.

Trustees—

The Very Rev. D. H. S. Cranage, M.A., Litt.D. (Dean of Norwich), C. R. A. Hammond, H. E. Witard, W. Hindes, Miss M. M. Clarkson, J. H. Dain, A. J. Cleveland, P. W. Jewson, R. Jewson, W. A. Riley, W. W. Williamson.

Clerk—Bernard H. L. Prior, D.S.O.

Steward—Bassett F. Hornor, D.S.O.

Chaplain—Rev. A. J. Andrews.   Master—E. Maidment.

Conditions for Admission.—Applicants must have resided in Norwich for three years before admission, and must be 65 years of age or over. Income from property must not exceed £12 a year; and applicants must be of good character.

Details of the Great Hospital in Bishopgate Street running between Riverside Road and the Cathedral.

The Lord Mayor and party went round the Great Hospital in Bishopgate [between the east end of the cathedral and Bishop Bridge] talking with the people there. Dr. Cleveland was chairman of the board of trustees of the Great Hospital, and J. H. Dain, the Chief Constable, was Vice-Chairman. The Sheriff that morning visited "the isolation hospital where the decorations were of red, white and blue."

The other place the Lord Mayor and the Sheriff went to was the Jenny Lind Children's Hospital situated in grounds on the corner of Unthank Road and Colman Road. Here, a report said "Christmas trees, holly and mistletoe made this hospital a perfect setting for the Lord Mayor in his civic robe of red, with gold chain and plumed tricorne hat. Little faces looked up in surprise as the red robed figure made its way through the wards where each cot had its share of dolls, toys, books and games. One little patient, round eyed with awe, whispered 'Is that the Archbishop?'"

That was not the end of the Lord Mayor's official duties that Christmas day in 1942, for in the afternoon he welcomed officers and men of the American Forces at the City Hall, and then paid a visit to the Norwich Lads Club in King Street [near where Mountergate meets King Street] for a special performance by the Blue Club Concert Party. The Lads Club was founded by John Dain in March 1918 for the purposes of bringing together working class lads for creative, social and sporting activities. The premises in King Street had a gym, billiard room, boxing ring and a stage for concert parties. There was also a St. John Ambulance group and the Lads Club band.

During the Christmas week the W.V.S. [Women's Voluntary Service] distributed to bombed out Norwich families over 600 parcels of "dried milk, sweetened cocoa, raisins, syrup, chocolate, toys and books, gifts received by the Lord Mayor of Norwich and the W.V.S. from Canada, North America and South Africa. There were also books and toys collected in this country for the bombed out children. Other parcels are to be distributed to children between the ages of three and five who have been evacuated to the country. Sent by the American Junior Red Cross, whose members have bought the contents with their own money, each parcel contains, among other things, a pair of gloves, a face flannel, soap, toothpaste, a doll and a paintbox."

In the *Eastern Evening News* of Friday1st January 1943, there appeared 'The Lord Mayor's New Year Message' with the first paragraph saying: 'The Lord Mayor (Dr. A. J. Cleveland) has consented to give a New Year message to the citizens of Norwich through the *Eastern Evening News*'. Here is an extract of the message.

"At the beginning of a New Year we are tempted to look forward, despite the fact that experience shows prophecy to be the most fallible of all mental activities. Though Norwich was one of the first cities in England to suffer air raids it was not until 1942 that we had our first experience of a real blitz.Terrifying and destructive as were the attacks on us during last summer they showed that we could 'take it' and that our preparations had been made with foresight and skill, and our plans carried out unselfishly and often with complete disregard of danger.

"Total war requires no condemnation. Its very acts condemn it as an insane and cruel method of settling differences. But even in the worst happenings there may be found some compensations. We have learnt, or should have learnt, lessons in this war which it will be folly to forget.

"As a nation we have never been so united. In our efforts to meet our perils side by side we have sunk all the petty distinctions of class and political creed, and we have found that neither clothes nor speech, nor wealth nor poverty can hide the true man or woman when human lives and the safety of our common citizenship are at stake.

"A great migration of our population has taken place. Town and country have got to know each other and appreciate each other's outlook. The gates of our charity have been opened wide, and everyone has shown a readiness to help wherever help is needed. In short, we have become good neighbours and good citizens."

THE SHERIFF OF NORWICH
(JOHN BROOKSBANK, J.P.)

Agent for Norwich Labour Party ; Secretary of the Norwich Trades
Council ; Member of Norwich City Council ; Chairman of the Norwich
Health Committee

The Sheriff of Norwich, Mr. John Brooksbank.

The Sheriff, John Brooksbank, also issued a New Year message which was printed in the *Eastern Daily Press* saying, amongst other things "Norwich, in common with many other parts of the country, suffered grievously this last year. It makes one proud to be associated with the city when one sees the people facing attack so courageously, applying themselves so unsparingly to aid the injured and save property both during and after a raid. They face the future, maybe without home or habitation, with calm and fortitude." He also talked about the future saying "I would specially urge that we all shall demand and prepare for the rebuilding of Norwich in the early post-war period on lines which will command the respects and thanks of coming generations: also that youth shall demand of politicians that the councils of the world shall take such steps as will eliminate the possibility of war in the future."

During the afternoon of Friday 1st January "an enemy raider dropped a stick of bombs" in the Derby Street [between Midland Street and Heigham Street] area of Norwich. A Mr. W. Westgate was walking in the street at the time was reported saying "We saw the plane come over, diving from the low clouds and almost touching the houses. Then the bombs began to drop and we got under a lorry. Directly after the bombs fell the plane started machine gunning."

Two houses collapsed after a bomb hit the rear of them, the occupants of one, a Mr. E. Bell and his mother and a dog, just managed to reach their shelter in the back garden in time. Nearby the Derby Arms public house was damaged as was a house on the opposite side of the road where a woman, her daughter, six young children and an eight month old baby "who had been burnt out of their home elsewhere" escaped to an Anderson shelter. One bomb hit St. Barnabas church in Russell Street. The *Eastern Daily Press* reported "There were no casualties beyond minor cuts from flying glass and in a few cases, slight shock."

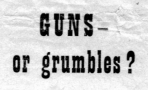

GUNS–
or grumbles?

Out of the pits come hundreds of thousands of tons of coal each day: fuel for the Battle of Fuel. Plenty for all in peace time. But *now*, there are a thousand new factories burning coal.

Which shall it be — the roaring fire at home or the hum of production in those factories?

What do I do...?

I work out my "target" allowance and budget my consumption of fuel.

I bear in mind that a two gallon bucket holds about 12 lbs. of coal or 8 lbs. of coke.

I read my gas and electricity meters, and measure my coal and coke, and I keep a weekly record of the fuel I use.

Issued by the Ministry of Information

Space presented to the Nation by the Brewers' Society

Careful use of coal was an important part of the war effort.

As Lord Mayor, Arthur Cleveland had to chair meetings of the Norwich City Council. Amongst the items on the agenda, for the 5th January meeting was the raising of fees at Norwich Cemetery as the cost of labour and maintenance had increased and there was a deficit in the funds. Also "The Council should agree to undertake until further notice the regular emptying of cesspools in the city [there were 162 remaining in the city at the time] without charge to the owner or occupier of the premises concerned at an annual estimated cost of £2810 and to purchase three cesspool emptiers at a cost of £942 each; that the Council should approve the education Committee's recommendation to buy furniture and equipment costing £560 for the expansion of the scheme for providing meals for children at school; and that £50 be allocated to the Norwich Publicity Association." But this latter request was turned down after "Mr. B. H. Clarke and Mr. Henderson had declared that the association did not propose to spend the money now, but to build up funds to renew a publicity campaign after the war. They claimed that to levy money from the citizens for something not needed now seemed absurd and that the association should wait until after the war."

The Lord Mayor, on Monday 11th January, presided over the annual meeting of the East Anglian Trustee Saving Bank at the Maids Head Hotel. The report said Dr. Cleveland "spoke of the great individualism which characterised the 19th century when this bank was founded and the danger of allowing our zeal for reform to outrun discretion in the changes that would follow the war. He hoped we would do everything possible to preserve the best of our individual work and not discard anything simply because it happened to be old. Destruction was not necessarily reconstruction."

At a meeting of the Norfolk War Savings Campaign Committee on Monday 18th January chaired by Herbert Gowen, a Norwich accountant, it was reported that since the campaign began in November 1939 ten and a half million pounds had been raised for the government. The secretary, Mr. J. W. Copeland, mentioned that the new savings centre on Guildhall Hill, opened at the beginning of November, and staffed by the volunteers, "during December had received over £3514, beating all previous records. There are now 718 savings groups in Norwich made up of: Street groups 374 (covering 408 streets), commercial and industrial 264, schools and school staffs 66, and social 14. It is estimated that 1000 voluntary workers are now actively engaged in the war savings campaign in Norwich"

The same day the Lord Mayor was at the opening ceremony at the Army Services Club in Palace Street [between Tombland and Cowgate] when Dr. Percy Herbert, the Bishop of Norwich, opened a new extension. The Bishop said, referring to the destruction of war, "that reconstruction must go on". The next day, Tuesday 19th, the Lord Mayor presided over the Police Court at the Guildhall. It was during his address there that he paid tribute to Alan Colman who had died two days before in a flying accident. First Officer Colman of the Air Transport Auxiliary was the second son of Russell Colman. Dr. Cleveland said "It seems hard that after being spared from the dangers of Dunkirk and the perils of a war-time journey to West Africa he should have lost his life in his own country. But there is no front line in this war, and Alan Colman died as much in battle as if he had been shot down by enemy action. Our deep sympathy goes out to the members of his family."

The Lord Mayor was often called upon to chair meetings of non-council organisations, such as the Norwich Decayed Tradesmen's Association's annual meeting at the Guildhall on Tuesday 26th January. The Association had been in existence for 150 years and had helped 7222 people, and over £43,500 had been distributed.

The next day the Lord Mayor welcomed six new magistrates at the Guildhall Police Court – Horace Allen, William Holt, Bassett Fardell, Francis Morse, Clifford Copeland and Mrs. M. Barclay. The Lord Mayor commented "They are all people well known in the city. Supt. H. W. Ball (Deputy Chief Constable of Norwich) assured the new magistrates of the loyalty of the city police. 'We shall do everything we can to assist them in the administration of the court' he said, 'and to see that everyone gets a square deal'" reported the *Eastern Daily Press*.

At the Council meeting on Tuesday 2nd February, the Lord Mayor congratulated those who received the M.B.E. for their services - Victor Harrison, a member of the Council and Chief Air Raid Warden, and Miss Lane, Matron of Norwich Maternity Home. Dr. Cleveland said "Mr. Harrison had done most valuable work in an entirely honorary post, and the honour he had gained was a recognition of that, and the services of those who worked under him." Of Miss Lane he said "All over this country where hospitals have suffered by the beastliness and horrors of this war, members of Miss Lane's profession have shown the utmost gallantry and devotion to duty. We in Norwich have been pretty badly hit in the hospital world; both at the Woodlands Hospital and the Norfolk and Norwich Hospital there were periods of extreme danger and I have heard nothing but praise for the ways the nurses stuck to their patients and helped them."

MR. VICTOR E. HARRISON, appointed Chief A.R.P. Warden in Norwich in succession to Capt. J. J. Chapman.

Victor Harrison, Chief A.R.P. [Air Raid Precautions] Warden for Norwich. Harrison was an independent cinema circuit owner with four cinemas in Norwich at the time, with others at Cromer, North Walsham and Aylsham.

Incendiary bombs during the raids of April 1942 had set fire to buildings in College Road [between Earlham Road and Unthank Road] of Norwich Training College, and on Saturday 13th February 1943 a ceremony of the opening of some temporary huts took place.

There that day were a number of dignitaries including the Bishop of Norwich, the Dean of Norwich, the Bishop of St. Edmundsbury and Ipswich, the Bishop of Ely, Canon F. A. Cockin, and the Lord Mayor of Norwich. Miss Duff, principal of the college, explained that they had "converted part of the old college school to become the new chapel and that the new building consisted of pre-fabricated concrete huts. 'We are very happy and comfortable in our new quarters' she added."

The report of the proceedings said that "Canon Cockin spoke as secretary to the Board of Supervision of Church Training Colleges saying that 'Some of those who composed the Board of Education's Committee strongly held the view that all teacher training should be done in a university setting, They failed to consider the contribution a training college can make in a particular area, such as Norwich provided'."

The report in the *Eastern Daily Press* also said that "The Lord Mayor in the course of some comments on education expressed the view that the object should be to teach us to think in an orderly way and how to behave. 'Your education should never cease' he observed. 'You are not educated when you leave school, and only partially educated when you end at three score years and ten'." The College moved in 1948 to Keswick Hall, on the outskirts of the city.

Another engagement in the Lord Mayor's busy diary was the presenting of prizes at the Blyth School Speech Day saying "that although the system of awarding prizes by examination results might not be perfect, it enabled one to produce knowledge at the moment it was needed." He went on to say that the school was more than a group of buildings and appealed to the girls to cultivate the school spirit, to be loyal to their school and companions and uphold a standard of decent behaviour. He then made a plea hoping that "The girls would take up nursing which was a vocation and not a trade or profession."

The headmistress, Mrs. F. E. Whitaker recounted that the Blyth School had received a direct hit the previous year, the gym being destroyed and parts of the main building damaged. "Through the kind co-operation through the heads of the Alderman Jex School and Angel Road School the girls had been able to take some of their lessons in a gymnasium."

On the Tuesday 16th February the Lord Mayor and Sheriff were at the Stuart Hall where "200 Jewish men in the Services were the guests at a reception to the Forces of the United Nations given by the Norwich Hebrew Congregation. The Lord Mayor said 'He was sure the occasion would result of a better appreciation of each other's qualities and points of view'." The Sheriff, John Brooksbank, "expressed his esteem for the Jewish people" a report in a local paper said, and that "his earnest hope that out of the present torment something better would emerge for the Jewry of the world." The report concluded with the sentence saying "A cabaret and dance music was provided by the Norfolk Turkeys."

Pigeons were released from each county of the country in the early afternoon of Saturday 20th February carrying a birthday greeting message to the Chief Guide, Lady Baden-Powell. The two carrier pigeons from Norfolk left the grounds of the Castle Museum with the message 'Thinking of our guide with affectionate greetings, thinking of our founder with deepest gratitude, thinking of our sisters the world over with continued admiration for their courage, and thinking of ourselves with humility and prayers that we maybe steadfast'. The report said "With Lady Somerleyton were the Lady Mayoress (Mrs. A. J. Cleveland), the President, and Mrs. Peacock, the

Divisional Commissioner. Mr. R. C. S. Rice assisted in despatching the pigeons." It was hoped the pigeons would reach their destination in London by 5 o'clock.

The Lord Mayor was also busy at the Castle that day looking at drawings and model aeroplanes made by members of the ATC in their spare time. "Some of the work was done by the Air Scouts, a new body now under the ATC, taking in boys from 11 to 15½" said a report in the *Eastern Daily Press.*

Norwich Salute: Red Army Day

ПРИВЕТ КРАСНОЙ АРМИИ

Бургомистр Норвича приветствует отважных бойцов британского союзника — Советского Союза. Норвич следит с восторгом за славным наступлением Красной Армии.

Вперед, вместе с союзниками, к победе над гитлеризмом!

TRANSLATION

The Lord Mayor of Norwich salutes the gallant soldiers of Britain's ally, Soviet Russia. Norwich watches with admiration the advance of the Red Army. Forward together to the United Nations' victory over Hitlerism.

ARTHUR J. CLEVELAND.

(See Notes by "Whiffler" on Page Three, about the Russian alphabet.)

On Sunday 21st February contingents from the armed forces and civil defence services from across the Eastern Region paraded through the streets of Cambridge to commemorate the entry of the Russian Army in the First World War. The Lord Mayor of Norwich and his civic party were there. Dr. Cleveland's message (left) was commented on by the columnist Whiffler in the Eastern Evening News *and included the following. "The type in which the translation of the Lord Mayor's message is printed was actually designed and cut in this country for the Russian Government. The Greek letters in the alphabet will present no difficulties to readers with a knowledge of either Greek or of mathematics. The shapes of certain of the letters of the Russian alphabet will be familiar enough, but for the English student the sounds they represent differ. For example, the Russian B is pronounced as an English V; the H as N; the P as R; the C as S; the X as CH in Scottish 'loch'. The Lord Mayor's message was translated by a Russian-speaking member of the 'Eastern Evening News' staff."*

The next day, Sunday 21st February, Dr. Cleveland with John Brooksbank the Sheriff, Bernard Storey the Town Clerk and Victor Harrison the Chief Warden, travelled to Cambridge to represent Norwich at the 25th anniversary of when the Russian Army began fighting in the First World War. The report said "It was on February 23rd 1918 that the Red Army first went into action against the Germans. Then Petrograd - or Leningrad, as it is now - was in danger. In commemoration of this fact Russia sets aside February 23rd to celebrate the Red Army's birthday each year. Every town or village in the counties of Norfolk, Suffolk, Essex, Bedfordshire,

Hertfordshire, Huntingdonshire and Cambridgeshire are represented in the parade through the streets."

Of the procession it said "The Army and the R.A.F. figured strongly in the picture and there were battalions of the Home Guard, the A.T.C., military cadets, and most of the civil war organisations. Units of women in the services, the Wrens, the A.T.S. [Auxiliary Territorial Service] - headed by the official A.T.S. band in the Army - the W.A.A.F. [Women's Auxiliary Air Force], hospital nurses and the Women's Land Army were singled out for special welcomes as the parade, a mile and a half in length, moved past.

"Sir John Anderson, with British and Russian officers, took the salute in front of the Fitzwilliam Museum." It went on to say that "One group of workers, twenty strong, had travelled from Norwich, and all had been selected from factories producing war help of the types Britain is supplying to Russia."

On Tuesday 23rd February six Canadian soldiers visited Great Yarmouth, and the next day, they toured round Norwich to see the city and a factory, and in the afternoon to an aerodrome in Norfolk. In the evening the Lord Mayor and Lady Mayoress gave them a dinner at the Royal Hotel. The purpose of this visit is not mentioned in the newspapers of the time, but the welcome was typical of Arthur Cleveland and his wife welcoming those from overseas.

Medical services and the Norfolk and Norwich Hospital were Dr. Cleveland's passions, and when he presided over the annual meeting of the Norwich District Nursing Association on Friday 26th February at the Guildhall he outlined his thinking. "There was too much overlapping and not enough co-operation in the system today he contended. There was need for more centralisation and more decentralisation. In each area there should be a specialist hospital staffed and equipped accordingly, and specialist work concentrated at it. This meant that much of the general work now undertaken at the large hospitals should be done at the smaller ones. Small injuries etc. that were now treated at the casualty department at the Norfolk and Norwich Hospital could be equally well seen after by a panel doctor or a district nurse. The medical profession referred all the cases it could to the panel doctor, but there was a strong tendency for all to go to the hospital, and a lot of work was done there un-necessarily. The panel system was started thirty years ago and needed to be reorganised to bring it in accordance with modern advances.

"There should be greater co-operation between the panel doctors, the hospitals and the district nurses" said the Lord Mayor. "I should like to see several posts in the city where your nurses could attend to dressings and give other minor treatment." He also referred to the many claims for charitable subscriptions that would continue after the war, and suggested that the Norfolk and Norwich War Charities Fund should be perpetuated in some form. "It had been so successful it could get more money for individual charities than was otherwise possible, and it ensured an equitable distribution."

Sunday, 28th February, both Arthur Cleveland and Evelyn Cleveland, along with the Sheriff John Brooksbank and his wife, were at the Norwich Philharmonic Society's concert to listen to, amongst other things, Beethoven's Fifth Symphony and 'a number of operatic arias sung by Miss Janet Hamilton-Smith and Mr. Henry Wendon'.

On Wednesday 3rd March 1943 readers of the *Eastern Daily Press* learnt that ratepayers in the city would be paying less. "Citizens will, we think, hardly need to be told that this 1s in the £ reduction in the rate is not the whole picture, though it is certainly the pleasantest and most welcome aspect of the actual state of the city's position. The reduction in rate revenue due to air raids just about balances the joint effect of the improved A.R.P. grants and the welcome reduction of the cost of social welfare grants. To round off the story we must remember that much work that would in peacetime figure in the estimates is necessarily being postponed during wartime, and that some day the arrears will have to be overtaken."

Part of the extensive Boulton and Paul's Riverside Works in Norwich. The factory site by the River Wensum can be located today using the Carrow Road football ground on the right of the picture as a reference point.

On the morning of Friday 5th March the Lord Mayor and Sheriff paid a visit to Boulton and Paul's works in Riverside Road. The company advertised themselves as 'Constructional steel engineers, manufacturers of portable buildings, iron fence and wire netting manufacturers'. This was the first in a series of visits by civic heads arranged by Arthur Cleveland as an encouragement to war workers to "assure them of their fellow-citizens appreciation of what they are doing to help on the war effort" said the local paper. The Managing Director of Boulton and Paul, Mr. J. Tresfon met the civic party on arrival, and with the

The Lord Mayor at Boulton and Pauls Riverside Works on Friday 5th March. Here he is inspecting the St. John Ambulance First Aid Unit. In the background is the Chief Constable, John Dain, and Managing Director J. F. Tresfon.

Chairman Mr. R. Jewson, and the directors Mr. S. Howes, Mr. G. Ffiske, Mr. H. Towlson and Mr. R. Taylor, then toured all departments to see the many manufacturing processes.

Boulton and Paul's war work was varied. Amongst the many small and large items they made were parts for radar installations, radio masts, steel and wooden buildings, large undercarriage frames for heavy tank transporters, flail attachments for tanks, special wire netting to be laid over grass or sand making runways strong enough for landing aircraft etc.

At the extensive Riverside Road works they made 85,400 Morrison air raid shelters - produced at one point at the rate of 2,500 a week. According to the 1947 Boulton and Paul book *The Leaf and the Tree* "All this work which Boulton and Paul undertook for the Second World War amounted to a turnover of something approaching £13,000,000."

The mayoral group looking round Riverside Works chatted with the men and women at their jobs - one of which was Deenie Cleveland, the Lord Mayor's daughter, who was a trained machinist who had been working in the factory's maintenance department for over a year.

The tour finished in the works canteen where the Lord Mayor spoke to a large gathering of employees. "Most people nowadays were doing something to bring the war to a successful conclusion, and the people helping in the factories were doing as much or more than many. They did not work in the limelight." He concluded by saying that his visit had enabled him to appreciate more than ever the value of their efforts, and on behalf of all the citizens he thanked them. The paper reported that "The Sheriff added his congratulations and said he was delighted to see the happy relationship existing between all."

The Lord Mayor watching one of the operators of the wire netting machine along with Mr. J. H. Tresfon (Managing Director), Mr. R. Taylor (Director), Mr. L. G. Hannaford (Director), and the Norwich Town Clerk Bernard Storey.

Women war workers made up a proportion of Boulton and Paul's staff. This is part of the wood working department.

Dr. Cleveland talking with a machine operator while on the left the Managing Director Mr. Tresfon, looks on.

The Lord Mayor watches his daughter, Deenie Cleveland, who was a trained machinist in the factory.

*The Sheriff, John Brooksbank, in Boulton and Paul's
canteen kitchen watching food being prepared.*

To get an idea of the sort of work one person was doing in the Boulton
and Paul factory in Riverside Road, Deenie Cleveland wrote later about her
work of 'Pinion Drilling'. "When I first went into an Engineering Workshop
I had not the smallest knowledge of the work I was about to undertake. I
knew I was to Pinion or deep hole drill, but what that meant I had not the
faintest idea. I had never before been in a factory, and my interests were
painting and music.

"I remember how shy and nervous I felt that first morning waiting
outside the foreman's office, and how I wondered if I should ever get used
to the noise or be liked by the people and become one of them. This latter
fear I soon found was uncalled for as I was shown nothing but kindness.

"Deep hole drilling is I think one of the few engineering jobs a woman
should be able to do better than a man, for it requires a light, delicate touch
and infinite patience, but no mathematical knowledge or heavy lifting. A
drill is a very easy machine to work, and once you have learnt your various
speeds and in the case of a belt driven drill, how to change your pulleys,
you have very little to worry about. When I first started drilling I could only
average 35 half-inch pinions a day, now I can do from 58–60 with time
spent on the Drill Grinder sharpening my own drills and those of other
drillers.

"I was lucky in being taught by a man full of humour. I learnt many
things during the years in the shop, but most useful of all was how to 'screw
my nut'. I shall never forget the first time I was told to do this and the time I

spent hunting for a nut to screw, and it was not until I told one of the old hands of my dilemma that I realised my mistake - amidst much laughter I learnt it meant to use your head."

During the morning of Saturday 6th March the Lord Mayor presided over the Norwich City Police Court when Gerald Hubbard was fined £1 with 3/- costs for a black-out offence at the Y.M.C.A. premises in St Giles, and A. H. Fisher, an RAF man returning home to 3 Pembroke Road [between Avenue Road and Park Lane] on February 21st found no one at home and that the property was without proper black-out facilities to stop light being visible. He was fined 5/- and 2/6 costs.

Miss May Sendall of Bignold Road [between Drayton Road and Appleyard Crescent] was in trouble after her dog 'flew up' and bit Mrs. E. Brown on the arm as she was passing Sendall's house on February 15th. Mr. Russell Steward, defending, "suggested that the Labrador retriever was excited at the time. On the evening in question the dog, which was usually kept on a chain, was let free to meet a member of the family who was expected home about that time. Christina Sendall, defendant's sister, said she had seen the dog jump at a woman once only, but it had not hurt her. On the particular evening when she saw complainant's arm had been injured by the dog, she offered to pay the expense of chemist's treatment. The bench ordered defendant to pay 12s 6d costs, with a warning that the dog had to be kept under control."

During the proceedings at the Guildhall the Lord Mayor presented a bronze medal and certificate to Stanley Pycroft of Alfordgrove, Sprowston, who stopped a runaway horse on Saturday December 19th in the Sprowston Road. "Not only has he saved probably several people from serious injury, but he also saved the life of a valuable animal" said Dr. Cleveland. The horse, belonging to the Co-op, was running down the centre of the road towards the city. The report stated that "the trailing shafts were striking its hind legs. He [Mr. Pycroft] ran beside the horse for a few yards and managed to grab the reins. He was dragged along the road, sliding on his feet, but eventually caused the animal to stop and turn round. The incident occurred when the milk cart to which the horse was attached came into collision with a motor lorry." The Norwich Co-operative Society presented the Lord Mayor with a £10 cheque.

In the afternoon the Lord Mayor chaired the annual meeting of the Norfolk Hospitals Contributors Association in the Council Chamber in the Guildhall. During the proceedings it was said that "during the last year subscriptions had been increased from 2d to 3d a week and that it had been possible to allocate £2000 to a contingency fund for additional aid to hospitals after the war."

Regarding the future Dr. Cleveland, "as chairman of the Norfolk and Norwich Hospital Board of Management knew the difficulties the hospital had to face at the end of the last war. It was the association, now the hospital's main support that had to come to their rescue. There was, he said, nothing new about the medical recommendations of the Beveridge Report, and a regionalisation of hospital services would probably have been carried through by now, but for the war."

The Lord Mayor's tour of Boulton and Paul's factory in Riverside Road concluded with a visit to the kitchen.

The report of the meeting in the *Eastern Daily Press* continued with Dr. Cleveland remarking on the Contributors Association that "I do not believe that as soon as the war is over the Government will carry through the Beveridge Report and close you down. I believe they will be glad to carry on for several years with the principles of voluntary support until the principles of State support are in full swing. I do not know if we shall be better off or not, but the services which we at the hospital have rendered to your members have been very good and will rank high in the standards of service for the country." Lastly he said that a new system at the hospital had been devised which would end "the dreary waiting in the out-patients department."

On Sunday morning, the 7th March, the Lord Mayor and a large audience of men and women of the Services, the Home Guard and cadets watched a special preview of the film *In Which We Serve* at the Regent Cinema in Prince of Wales Road. "Before the performance the uniformed men and women and boys marched past a saluting base to the music of the 9th Royal Norfolk Home Guard, a senior officer of the Royal Norfolk Regiment taking the salute." *In Which We Serve* starred Noel Coward, John Mills, Celia Johnson, Michael Wilding and a host of familiar actors of the time. It was released in October 1942 and told the story of a torpedoed British destroyer in flashbacks with much emphasis on the camaraderie of the wrecked crew. The film was shown at the Regent for the week beginning Monday 8th March.

Norwich theatres and some of the cinemas for the week beginning Monday 8th March 1943. From the leader page of the Eastern Daily Press.

The *Eastern Daily Press* announced on 10th March 1943 that "Mothers of growing children may find an answer to the clothes problem in Norwich W.V.S. clothing exchange, which opens at the London Street depot today from 2.30 to 5pm. Clothes taken for exchange must be clean and in good condition. They will be given a points value, and the owner will receive a voucher to exchange for other articles assessed at an equal number of points. No coupons will be required."

On Saturday 13th March the Lord Mayor opened an exhibition of Czechoslovakian Arts and Crafts at the Castle Museum. Dr Cleveland said "One of the best ways of becoming friends with a nation is through an understanding of its culture." Paintings, some showing air raid scenes and some abstract, by members of the Czechoslovak forces hung by examples of people's needlework and caps made in the 19th century worn by "married women in the intimacy of their homes. There are also embroidered blouses and other dress accessories showing variety in technique and design. The exhibition on the whole, though small, gives a general idea of ancient and modern Czechoslovakia, as well as the part the country is playing in the preset war" said a report in the *Eastern Daily Press*.

Evelyn Cleveland, wife of the Lord Mayor, presided over a meeting on Monday 15th March, along with Vice President Mrs. Brooksbank, wife of the Sheriff, concerning arrangements for a collection to take place on May 15th - subject to the approval of the Watch Committee - for the Alexandra Rose Day Collection. The same day Herbert Gowen, chairman of the Norwich Savings Committee, was at a meeting to organise the Wings For Victory Week to take place from May 22nd to May 29th, when it was hoped to raise £100,000. "The £100,000 which the city will be asked to raise will provide the following aircraft: Three Sunderlands (£50,000 each), 16 four-engine bombers (£40,000 each), 15 twin-engine fighters (£8,000 each), 18 single-engine fighters (£5000 each)." The same day Miss Denise Farquharson, organising secretary of the Norfolk War Charities Committee, said at a meeting that they were giving £500 towards a fund for providing bicycles to soldiers stationed on rural sites. "An appeal for money to buy bicycles for A.A. units [Anti Aircraft] in order that men stationed in isolated districts can enjoy short periods off duty, was made to the Norwich Rotary Club by the honorary colonel of a searchlight regiment. The appeal was passed on to the committee. The Rotary Club has in addition, subscribed £15 and the colonel £50."

The *Eastern Daily Press* reported on the 19th March that just before midnight of Thursday [18th March] "high explosives and a large number of incendiaries, many of them of the explosive type, were dropped in several localities and some damage was caused to civilian property. Several bursts of machine gun fire were heard. A number of people had to be evacuated from their homes and invaluable assistance was rendered to the Civil Defence services by troops stationed in the area. There were no fatal casualties, but three persons had to be admitted to hospital, one of them seriously hurt. Many of the bombs were of the explosive canister type, throwing out phosphorous projectiles, which have come to be known as 'flower pots' among the A.R.P. workers." According to Joan Banger in her

Norwich at War published by Poppyland Publishing [2nd edition 1989] "considering the number of bombs that were dropped the damage caused was remarkably slight." The main casualty was Harmer's clothing factory in St. Andrews Street, hit again, and this time virtually burnt out. Here they had made uniforms for the Armed Forces and Civil Defence.

Result of an air raid on Norwich on Thursday 18th March 1943.
Harmer's clothing factory in St Andrews Street burnt out.

Having lived close to Thorpe Station for many years, Arthur Cleveland seemed to have an interest in railways and trains. So when he and the Sheriff John Brooksbank were invited to look round the L.N.E.R. [London and North Eastern Railway] premises on Wednesday 24th March they were eager visitors. The Lord Mayor began in the "telegraph room where he was handed a greetings telegram from headquarters of the L.N.E.R.", and the Sheriff got to drive "a turntable on which was a 126 ton locomotive and worked the machinery which completely lifted a wagon of coal and tipped the contents into a conveyor."

The civic was shown the different types of steam locomotives, signalling and engineering shops. "The Lord Mayor showed a special interest in the number of women working in the repair and cleaning shops and one girl who explained to him the intricacies of cleaning said she liked the work very much. In another shop a girl fitter explained that she had been working at the bench for twenty weeks following a training course of eight weeks."

Manthorpe's grocery shop at No. 8 White Lion Street specialised in health foods, so perhaps these biscuits were available there.

War-time cookery demonstrations were held at the W.V.S. premises in London Street on Thursday March 25th and Friday 26th at 3.15pm each day. What these entailed is not recorded, but the newspapers carried food and cooking hints issued by the Ministry of Food regularly, and short Food Facts films appeared in the cinemas telling people such things as how to eat a herring and not to waste bread. Also at the W.V.S. centre the *Eastern Daily Press* mentioned "working parties for slipper making for rest centres are to be held on Mondays at 3pm at the depot."

The *Eastern Evening News* of Saturday 27th March reported a meeting in Suckling Hall [next to what is now Cinema City] of the Norfolk and Norwich branches of the College of Midwives of which the most important agenda item was the proposed amalgamation of the Norwich Municipal Maternity Home and the County Group. After some discussion it was agreed to go ahead. The Lord Mayor who was present spoke of the need for co-operation and co-ordination of the present hospital, medical and other public health services.

At St. Peter Mancroft Hall on Monday 29th March the annual public meeting of the Mid-Norfolk Branch of the N.S.P.C.C. [National Society for the Prevention of Cruelty to Children] was held at which the Lord Mayor presided. Also in attendance was Mrs. Cleveland, and the Sheriff Mr. J. W. Brooksbank. According to the report in the *Eastern Daily Press* Dr. Cleveland "spoke of the influence of the home in a child's background. Decent houses and education, food, and clothing were necessary, but a house did not of necessity make a home. He felt a great many young women were not being properly brought up to be mothers and wives. 'We do not want a standardised nation; we want a bond of sympathy between parent and child'."

At the Grammar School playing field in the Lower Close on Saturday 3rd April following earlier rounds of the Rugby Services teams, the Lord Mayor kicked off the final match. "In the final 'B' team by clever forward work held the speedy threequarters for most of the game, but good passing movements, in the later stages gave 'A' team the verdict of two goals and a try (13 points) to nil." The Lord Mayor then presented a silver cup to the winners.

In the midst of all this going on, and the war on Norwich's doorstep as it were, it is surprising that Norwich City Council was thinking about moving the cattle market out of the city centre. Every Saturday the city was crowded with small-holders, farmers and stockmen and other county folk going to the livestock market filled with sheep, poultry pigs, and cattle – some of the latter having walked on the hoof to Norwich from the countryside. There were also stalls and farm machinery on display. The cattle market was right in the centre of Norwich just below the Castle, filling a wide open space between the Agricultural Hall [now ITV Anglia], Rose Lane and Farmers Avenue.

With the Lord Mayor presiding on Tuesday 6th April, Norwich City Council decided in principle on a recommendation to move, after the war, the cattle market and all that went with it out to a new 55 acre site west of the city at Harford. This was seen as an improvement as part of a scheme of reconstruction for the city, though there were those who were against the idea - including the Lord Mayor. The voting was thirty for the move, and twenty against. Actually the Market Committee came up with the idea for a move in 1938, but other things had intervened.

Nothing much happened to the proposed move to Harford for a very long time - the move not taking place until 1960. This then left the large former cattle market site by the castle redundant, it being used mainly as a car park and for the annual fair. Later the site was cleared, an archaeology dig took place, and a new shopping complex built and opened in 1993 called Castle Mall, now known as the Castle Quarter.

On Saturday, the 10th April 1943 at 3pm, the Lord Mayor officially opened an Army Exhibition at the Castle Museum. This consisted of some Army equipment including a Sten gun, Tommy-gun and a new type of three-inch mortar gun. There were models of tank landing craft and paratroops and their equipment. There were lots of photographs on show including "men advancing under fire, 'attack commandos moving forward to assault', Scots Guards at El Alamein, 'cold steel', and 'A soldier of the fighting vanguard'." There was also a photograph of Mr. Stather Hunt, son of the Rector of Pakefield, guarding German prisoners.

In his speech the Lord Mayor said "that although Norwich had adopted the H.M.S. Norfolk and a squadron of the R.A.F., they had not adopted a unit of the Army. The city took a personal interest in the Royal Norfolk Regiment, the 9th Foot, whose military history was second to none, and the Norfolk Yeomanry, who had long established a reputation for efficiency and bravery." The exhibition was open all week at the Castle Museum, from 10am to 5pm. Admission was free.

The *Eastern Daily Press* reported on 17th April that "The Pilot officers from Australia and New Zealand who are touring this part of England, were received by Mr. Herbert P. Gowen, an ex-Lord Mayor [1928-29] and Chairman of the Norwich Publicity Association, when they visited Norwich." In the evening Dr. Cleveland and Mrs. Cleveland entertained the Airman to a dinner. On the Sunday they went to the Cathedral, and looked round a factory where they were given lunch.

Monday 26th April the Lord Mayor was at Carrow Road football ground in the afternoon to see the first inter-league match between Norwich and Ipswich junior teams. "With Mayes a clever leader, the Ipswich forwards combined well and looked dangerous when attacking, but Norwich defended stoutly." The result was a draw - Norwich 2, Ipswich 2. "During the interval the Lord Mayor (Dr. A. J. Cleveland) presented the three Norwich League trophies to the winners, C.E.Y.M.S. [Church of England Young Men's Society football club] and Norman (2)."

The next day, Tuesday 27th April, the Lord Mayor was at the Stuart Hall where he introduced Mr. Hsieh, a graduate from Yenching University in Peking who gave a talk on Anglo-Chinese Relations. A report in the *Eastern Daily Press* of the talk included: "Although importance of reopening the Burma Road was not fully recognised by Allied High Commands, the speaker said he would be doing a disservice to Britain if he did not voice the disappointment of the Chinese people who were hoping for a greater amount of equipment and supplies than had been sent since the closing of the Burma Road" said Mr. Hsieh, who then went on to say "However much we may hope from political and economical development in the post-war years, we could not hope for completely satisfactory relationships if we failed to bring our two minds together and to bring our two peoples together in the cultural field." Commenting on the scheme of sending Chinese students to study in England, he said he "hoped the day would come when the West would reciprocate by sending students to China. I do not pretend we have anything valuable to offer in the field of science, but perhaps in our philosophy, art and literature here is still something which the West might find useful for its future." A vote of thanks was given by the Sheriff, Mr. Brooksbank. The talk had been organised by Helen Colman of the Norwich University Extension Society.

The 171st report of the Board of Management of the Norfolk and Norwich Hospital and the Norfolk and Norwich Eye Infirmary, presented at the Annual General Meeting on Saturday 1st May 1943, said that 1942 was probably the most difficult year in the history of the hospital. "The total number of in-patients admitted during the year was 6460, a decrease of 523, and the daily average number of beds occupied was 217 as compared with 280. The total of 21,906 new out-patients was 735 less than in 1941. Income came to £79,975 and expenditure £79,706. Receipts from the Contributors Association were £46,230 (an increase of £6950), legacies totalled £4750 and donations £2516." The Vice-Chairman, Mr. C. R. Hammond, said that the accounts at present showed "a pretty picture", but that did not take into account four years of no repairs or renewal of equipment through loss or wearing out.

Dr. Cleveland "spoke of the difficulties of administration entailed by the hospital beds being distributed in four places - 50 at Thorpe, 50 at Attleborough, 80 at Drayton, and about 180 in Norwich - and said in addition it had been most difficult to keep the domestic staff up to strength. The burden put on the medical officers and staffs had been very heavy and all deserved high praise for the way they had shouldered it.

"The emergency medical service was founded on the voluntary hospitals; the government had never hesitated to make demand after demand upon it and that in itself was a high testimony to the efficiency of an organisation which some said was out of date. If today they were writing the last chapter in the history of voluntary hospitals then they could claim it was the finest of all."

Dr. Cleveland had been Chairman of the Board of Management since 1938, and now retired from that role. The report of the meeting noted the "exceptional service rendered to the hospital by Dr. Cleveland, especially as chairman of the Board of Management for the past five years, and it was decided to elect him a vice-president." Richard Jewson, one of the Vice-Presidents, said "Dr. Cleveland had given voluntary service to the hospital for nearly forty years. That service had been outstanding because of his great natural gifts and ability. They did not elect their president – he was selected for them by the King, and they were peculiarly fortunate in his Majesty's present selection – but they did elect their vice-presidents, and they could do Dr. Cleveland no greater honour than by asking him to hold that office. Mr. Colman [Russell Colman, President] spoke of Dr. Cleveland's double responsibility as Lord Mayor and head of the hospital management, and also expressed admiration of the members of the staff who worked for the safety of the patients during the air raids heedless of the risk from falling bombs."

A proposal, at a meeting on Tuesday 4th May of the Norwich City Council under the chairmanship of the Lord Mayor, from the Health Committee, was the suggestion to appoint a person "to give practical instruction to cases from time to time under the consideration of the Health Sub-committee re unsatisfactory households" at £4 per week. The vote was in favour 25 to 18. "The terms and conditions and selection of candidate were left in the hands of Miss Clarkson, Mrs. High and Mrs. Fugill, who are members of the sub-committee." Another decision by the General Purposes Committee was to hire a house – No. 11 Harvey Lane owned by Boulton and Paul – "for use as accommodation for infirm patients, required as a result of air raid damage to the Woodlands Hospital." The council also passed a proposal from John Brooksbank "that the standard figure for domiciliary assistance payable to unemployable and other necessitous blind persons should be increased to 35s [£1.15.0] per week, with corresponding increase in the rest of the scale, as from May 19th next. A supplementary estimate for £2000 was made to provide for the additional cost in the present financial year."

```
════════════════════════════════════════
    BLACK-OUT 7.15 p.m. to 6.56 a.m.
SUN  RISES      7.29 a.m.      SETS    6.45 p.m.
MOON  RISES   8.44 a.m        SETS    9.32 p.m.
              First  Quarter—March  13th.
              Sets  2.4  a.m.      Rises  11.10  a.m.
              Full  Moon—March  21st.
              Sets  7.10  a.m.      Rises  6.48  p.m.
              Last  Quarter—March  29th.
Rises  ···   2.58 a.m.         Sets  ...  11.42  a.m.
   First  Quarter—April  4th
Rises  ...   6.44 a.m.         Sets  ...    7.7   p.m.
   High  Water—Yarmouth,  11.20  a.m.  and  11.34
p.m.   Lowestoft,  11.44  a.m.       King's  Lynn,
8.48 a.m.  and  9.4  p.m.    Cromer,  9.8  a.m.  and
9.24  p.m.
        LIGHTING-UP  TIME,  7.15  p.m.
```

Every day the local paper announced the blackout times and the phases of the moon - which helped when the sky was clear and there was a full moon to see one's way about. This is from the Eastern Daily Press *of Monday 8th March 1943.*

In the dark, early hours of Wednesday 5th May "the north-west perimeter of the City was suddenly lit by flares and shortly afterwards phosphorous and explosive incendiary bombs rained down" recorded Joan Banger in her book *Norwich at War*. This resulted in fires in St. Andrews Street, Cadge Close, Earlham Green Lane and Dereham Road. Joan Banger wrote "All the bombs on this estate exploded but happily all were extinguished by wardens and fireguards. A further nine phosphorus and nine incendiary bombs fell on Bunkers Hill Wood in Larkman Lane and exploded." In the centre of the city a bomb exploded in Exchange Street damaging the water mains and leaving a six feet crater, and outside St Michael-at-Plea church in Queen Street an incendiary bomb came down but failed to explode and was later removed. There were no serious casualties, just three people slightly hurt.

The Lord Mayor was busy on the evening of Thursday 6th May when a thousand Boy Scouts from 30 troops lined up in The Close and were inspected by the Lord Mayor before attending a service in the Cathedral where they were joined by 'Girl Guide Officers'. Outside the west door "A score of colour-bearers formed a guard of honour and before the service opened the colours were received by Archdeacon Moore and Canon Lanchester. The service was in memory of Lord Baden Powell, Chief Scout, who had died two years before."

The Lord Mayor presided over a meeting on Sunday 9th May at the Citadel in St Giles, at which Colonel Carvosso Gauntlett spoke of the Salvation Army as a League of Nations. The speaker had visited most of the countries where the Salvation Army worked and at the Citadel in St Giles spoke about the work they were doing of which he had experience of over the past 30 years. "Pointing out that the Salvation Army had already established a League of People long before there was a United Nations, the Colonel remarked that Salvationists were rather proud of the fact that theirs was the only flag which flies on both sides of the battle front. He urged the necessity of learning another language in addition to English as a step towards understanding other people" reported the *Eastern Daily Press*.

The aim of the Wings For Victory week was to raise
£1,000,000. In fact Norwich raised £1,456,363.

Raising funds for the war effort was a continuing job, and the *Eastern Evening News* of Thursday 13th May reported that regular house-to-house collections were being made for the Norwich War Charities Fund. The Lord Mayor and Sheriff attended a meeting at the Stuart Hall organised to increase the amount given, setting a target of £500 per month. "Miss J. Ruscoe, deputy organising secretary of the fund, said 'We have now completed our organisation to cover the whole of Norwich, dividing the city into the municipal wards, each of which has its own organiser. At present we have some 300 collectors, but to cover every street we need double that number'. To make her job a success each collector should organise it so that she knew when all or most of the people from whom she collected would be at home and thereby avoid fruitless calls through householders being out'. Mrs. J. R. Willis, honorary organiser of the house-to-house collections said 'That with few exceptions people were quite willing to give regularly to the fund once they had been approached'" said the *Eastern Daily Press*.

On Sunday16th May "Thousands of people saw at first hand just how well the Home Guard has prepared itself during the last three years" as they marched past City Hall watched by the Lord Mayor and Sheriff and an Army Divisional Commander who took the salute. "Public confidence in

A Lancaster bomber taking off from a Norfolk aerodrome.
From the Wings For Victory programme, drawn by Roy Nockolds.

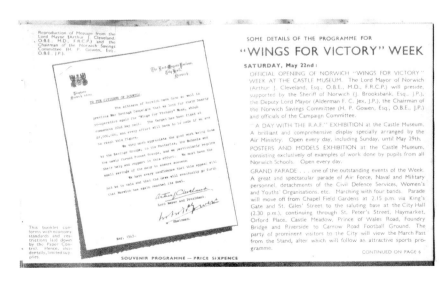

The Introduction in the Wings For Victory programme.

our great citizens army has developed as rapidly as its ranks have expanded, and if anything was needed to inspire that confidence still further it was provided by the birthday parade of the two well-equipped Norwich battalions. They later proved their efficiency in demonstrations of their striking powers, with a variety of weapons" said the local newspaper. These celebrations three years after the formation of the Home Guard took place all over the country, and in London King George VI watched a parade of over 5000 Home Guard members in Hyde Park.

There were all sorts of fund raising activities going on both nationally and locally. The *Eastern Daily Press* of Monday 17th May reported that "At one of the schools in District 6 the scholars, who are only eight years old, have set themselves a target of one guinea. One little girl has taken a doll to the school, and the children are paying a ½d to guess its name, the one who has it right to have the doll." This was followed by a letter in the paper on the 19th May saying "I was very concerned to see in the EDP on Monday a report of efforts in connexion with Norwich 'Wings For Victory' week which included an account of a child raffling a doll at school. One of the most pressing reforms needed in the country is a decrease in the gambling craze, and the schools should be adding their weight on the side of a sensible and responsible use of money. This is a much bigger matter than the subscription of halfpence to good causes and I hope steps will be taken to prevent any recurrence of this kind of thing."

Wings For Victory Week began on 22nd May. On the City Hall steps are:

Back row:
H. G. Strauss MP   Sir G. Shakespeare MP   Colonel Tozer C.B.E.   Captain Harold Balfour   Bernard Storey – Town Clerk

Middle row:
Major General Hodges USAA.   Major General Ozanne C.B.E.   Under Secretary of State for Air
Admiral Sir Dudley North

Front:
John Brooksbank, Sheriff   The Lord Mayor facing to the left

Go to the

"WINGS FOR VICTORY"
BALL
SAMSON & HERCULES HOUSE

Under the patronage of the Lord Mayor, Lady Mayoress, and the Sheriff

7.30 p.m. Wednesday, May 26th

THREE BANDS—

R.A.F. Swingtette, Czechoslovak Orchestra, Samson & Hercules Resident Dance Band

Tickets **5/-** each. Obtainable from the Norwich Savings Centre, Guildhall Hill, or Willmotts Stores, Prince of Wales-rd., Norwich

"WINGS FOR VICTORY" WEEK
NORWICH, MAY 22nd—29th

Space generously contributed by Norvic Shoe Co., Ltd.

WINGS *for* VICTORY

Wings For Victory special event during the evening of the 26th May.

The Wings For Victory week officially began on Saturday May 22nd although some people had begun collecting already. The idea was to raise a large amount of money towards planes for the RAF. It was a busy week, and Monday 24th was also Empire Day. The Lord Mayor decided to revive civic visits to schools in Norwich. Accompanied by the Lady Mayoress and Mr. E. W. Woodhead, Director of Education, they went to the City of Norwich School and an un-named girl's elementary school. The Deputy Mayor and the Sheriff went to other schools including the Blyth Secondary School. This was a time when even school children were helping to raise money towards the war effort. The City of Norwich School had already raised £1370 during Warships Week. The morning of the Lord Mayor's visit the boys raised within two hours £100 by buying certificates and stamps. The Lord Mayor not only thanked everyone, but admired the boys drawings of saving posters displayed for all to see.

People and businesses were generous in donating money towards winning the war as we have seen. Employees 'of a boot and shoe factory' raised 25 guineas, and the Norwich Union gave £250,000. In Boulton and

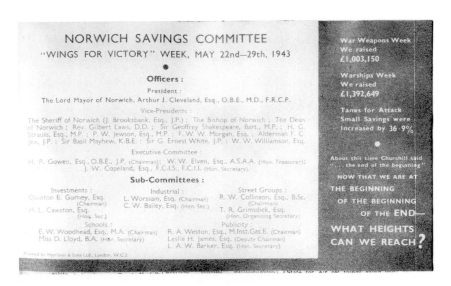

A page from the Norwich Wings For Victory programme.

Paul's canteen Mrs. E. M. Ettersbank ran daily competitions. "The lunch-hour competition produced £51 on Saturday, £50 on Monday and a similar amount yesterday" reported the *Eastern Daily Press* on 26th May. "In Garlands [a fashion & drapery store in London Street] 'Wings' window display are attractive models of planes which will be sold to the highest bidders. Sealed boxes have been placed in the shop in which offers for the models can be placed."

Amongst the companies raising funds for the war effort a savings group within Harry Pointer Ltd. [haulage contractors] in Guardian Road "invested £689", and employees of James Southall & Co. [boot manufacturers in Crome Road, off Mousehold Avenue] also helped generously. "In the closing room 200 girls have invested £1300, in the making room 185 men and girls have invested £900, and the staff of 85 have saved £650 this week. The weeks total so far for the firm's employees is £3,100, which, with investments by directors, brings the firm's figure to £6,700."

On a smaller scale six boys in Mile Cross Lane - R. Humphreys, B. Jones, A. and L. Hunton, A. Holmes and B. Thompson - raised £2.3.0 "towards a bomber to bomb Hitler - good luck to the pilot", and seven school children who "took over a blitzed house in Pelham Road [between St. Clements Hill and Catton Grove Road] have made a miniature stores for articles they collected and already raised £10. They plan personally to present a free victory gift to the Lord Mayor."

Dealing with the money given was a task carried by the Norwich Post Office, which not only counted the "thousands of threepenny pieces [which] have poured in" but bags bulging with sixpences and copper coins. "This tells you why there has been a shortage of small change just lately."

The Lord Mayor and Lady Mayoress at an unknown school somewhere in Norwich.

The Norwich Post Office acted as a "clearing house for savings certificates, savings stamps, and Post Office deposits. The staff working at speed for 12 hours a day sitting among big piles of Treasury notes and money bags, meticulously checking every halfpenny, stamp and voucher." An official at the Post Office said that "Many of the packets of notes we are having to handle are strong with the smell of camphor [moth balls]. They must have reposed in linen boxes with the passions of housewives for quite a while".

Tuesday 25th May, the day of the 145th Annual General Meeting of the Norwich Union Fire Insurance Society. "As usual I will deal with the Fire account first" said the Chairman, Ernest Hicks. "There is, you will notice, a satisfactory increase of £122,050 in premium income, and a gratifying profit of £204,261 is available for transfer to the Profit and Loss account. Taxation in the Dominions and in foreign countries from which we still derive business is again heavy, mainly due to war necessities, and has resulted in a substantial charge against Underwriting. There is no immediate prospect of any diminution in these demands, which must of necessity be taken as part of the sacrifices to be made under the conditions now existing. Although in the early months of 1942 extension of hostilities involved practically the whole world in the war, I am glad to say this extension has not further affected the Society beyond the point mentioned in my previous address."

He mentioned that the total assets of the Society now stood at £8,151,839. Of the minor things he spoke of was that the Norwich Union's own buildings which were damaged in the raids of 27th April 1942, and in an earlier raid which destroyed an office block behind the Fire Office building in Surrey Street. Of the Society's men in the services, nine had been killed or were missing during the last year, bringing the total since the war began to twenty one.

This Norwich Union advert appeared in the Norwich Annual *for 1943.*

Also that day there was the 135th Annual General Meeting of the Norwich Union Life Insurance Society. At that time the Life Insurance Society and the Fire Insurance Society operated as separate organisations, although of course all part of the same Norwich Union. The meeting, very similar to the Fire Insurance one, laid out the present situation. Dr. Cleveland attended as a member of the Board. At the meeting the President, Ernest Hicks, said "For the first time for many years – indeed for the first time since the last war – I have to report a small loss on mortality. Our total claims for the year were £1,356, 536, and these included the large sum of £213,000 due to war deaths at home and abroad. This is regrettable from many points of view, but must be regarded as a further direct contribution by the Society to the Nation's needs."

Mr. Hicks also referred to the problems of carrying on in war time, when he said "the inside staffs had been reduced to a minimum. We now have nearly 350 members of the Head Office and Home Branch staffs serving in the Forces of the Crown, in all parts of the world, in addition to the many men from overseas who have rallied to the call, either of the Home Country or of their own Dominion, to whom we wish a safe and speedy return, though I much regret that we have lost during the year four more of our promising young men, all members of the Royal Air Force, and you will wish to join with me in expressing our most sincere sympathy with their relatives and friends." Because of the shortage of staff those remaining at Norwich often worked hard late into the evening dealing with letters and enquiries, and then going on to do civil defence work.

The Norfolk News Company's offices were in London Street with the printing works behind and the distribution area pouring out into St. Andrews Hill Lane.

After other matters the Lord Mayor spoke on behalf of the directors. He referred, as the *Eastern Daily Press* reported, to "the Beveridge Report [of 1942] which was designed to guarantee against every contingency from the cradle to the grave, he said he hoped people would realise, as Sir William Beveridge most certainly did, that the first point about an insurance policy was that you must be able to pay the premium. The importance of sustaining our industries, works and undertakings must be borne in mind in formulating our post-war plans, for without means of livelihood for our citizens there would be no money to provide the amenities."

It is interesting to note that the chairman of both the Fire Society and Life Society, Ernest Hicks, a solicitor by profession, who had been on the board of the Life Society since 1930, and its chairman since 1935, retired at that meeting on 25th May. Sir Robert Bignold was elected the new chairman. To make the two Society's boards identical, it was decided that Dr. Cleveland, who was already on the Life Society board, should also be made a director of the Fire Office.

Back to the Wings For Victory Week. Friday 28th May the *Eastern Daily Press* was able to announce that the recent fund raising centred around the week had passed the million pound target. The newspaper published a letter from Arthur Cleveland, the President, and Herbert Gowen, the Chairman. "We desire to express our thanks to all those who have so readily contributed to make our Week such a success. Although we have reached the £1,000,000 mark we hope that this fact will not induce the citizens to relax their efforts, but rather will spur them on to further achievements, and to subscribe to the various Government Loans as freely as possible. We should like everybody in, or connected with, the Royal Air Force to feel that

On Saturday 12th June 1943 King Peter of Jugoslavia visited the Head Office of the Norwich Union Life Insurance Society in Surrey Street and had lunch there. On the steps are left to right: W. W. Williamson - Norwich Union Life Society General Manager, John Brooksbank – Sheriff of Norwich, King Peter of Jugoslavia, Dr. S. Budisavljevitch, General Radovitch, Sir Robert Bignold (who hosted the lunch), the Bishop of Norwich - Dr. P. Herbert, Bernard B. Riviere, and Dr. Arthur Cleveland - the Lord Mayor of Norwich. King Peter was wearing the uniform of a Lieutenant Colonel of the Jugoslav Infantry. Note that Dr. Cleveland has a cigarette in his right hand, and Sir Robert Bignold a cigar.

the people of Norwich are appreciative of their great work and intend to do everything possible to see that they have sufficient planes to carry out their job to a successful issue. Many of us have no other opportunity of expressing our thanks to them. Every shilling helps." The final total of Norwich's Wings For Victory campaign was £1,456,363.

Saturday June 5th was Buttercup Day in Norwich. This was supported by the Lady Mayoress, the idea being to raise funds for the Royal National Orthopaedic Hospital for the Cure of Crippled Children. Groups around the city were organised and £557 was raised. "Thanks are due to the many sellers who worked with such energy and enthusiasm and to the public who gave so generously for their buttercups in spite of the many other calls which are made on them in these difficult times."

In June King Peter of Jugoslavia came to Norwich to open an exhibition at the Castle Museum. Similar exhibitions had been held in other parts of

Also an exhibition in premises in Rampant Horse Street to raise money for the War Charities Fund was opened by the Lord Mayor on Wednesday 16th June.

the country, the idea being "to give some idea of the activities of the countries Britain extended hospitality to when the Axis Powers strangled liberty" reported the *Eastern Daily Press* on Monday 14th June. "In arranging the exhibition Norwich doubtless wished to express sympathy for his people, who threw in their lot with Britain at a moment when almost everything seemed lost. Britain had not forgotten the resistance of Jugoslavia for two years." The King remarked "The Nazi-Fascist monster is losing its breath and, with trepidation, awaits the mortal blow, to be delivered in the near future by the armies of the United Nations."

The exhibition consisted of sculptures, metal craftsmanship, embroidered dresses in traditional design, paintings, drawings and photographs giving a look into the country, its industries and people. King Peter, accompanied by the Lord Mayor, visited the City Hall, the Norwich Services Club, and the Norwich Union offices where the party had lunch.

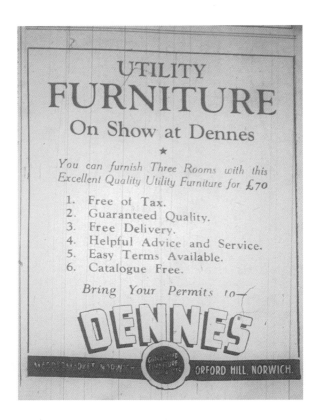

They also visited Colman's Carrow works where King Peter met the Lord Lieutenant of Norfolk, Mr. Russell Colman.

Another exhibition, this time giving people an idea of what was happening on the various war fronts, was opened by the Lord Mayor, accompanied by Mr. Brooksbank and Sir Basil Mayhew (one of the Vice-Presidents of the Norwich Savings Committee), in premises in Rampant Horse Street on the 16th June. In this War Charities shop, on two floors, there were maps, photographs, and original copies of underground newspapers published in France, Poland, Belgium, Norway and other occupied countries. There was also a section devoted to Norfolk men and women serving at home and abroad. Upstairs war news films were shown. The exhibition also featured 'Joe Penny'- a picture of a man in overalls – symbolising 'the penny in every £' aim of the Norfolk and Norwich War Charities Fund. Visitors, when leaving the exhibition, could drop a penny or two into "a receptacle provided."

On 19th June the Lord Mayor presented the Royal Humane Society's testimonial on vellum to Ronald Spalls of Gipsy Close, Norwich. Spalls, along with some other boys, were playing by the Wensum, close to Carey's Boathouse in Heigham Street, on 18th April, when 5 year-old Brenda

Cozens fell into the water. "Without hesitation Spalls dived into the river fully clothed and swam to the child twenty yards away" said the testimonial. Getting to the bank another boy helped get them out of the river which at this point was between five and twelve feet deep. "The child after artificial respiration and first aid treatment appeared little worse for her immersion."

The Lord Mayor said to Spalls "You grasped the situation at once and did what was the right thing to do. You are making a good start in life, and I hope you will add to your good qualities what all brave people possess – modesty."

On Monday June 21st the Lord Mayor opened an unusual exhibition, this time in the Stuart Hall. Sixteen stores had got together to put on a show of the latest utility furniture available. The local paper said that "The furniture is made of timber and hardboard veneered and has a matt wax finish. Light and dark oak and some mahogany are employed, and all the designs harmonise, so that suites are interchangeable. Housewives will note with satisfaction that the wardrobes (which are fitted with long mirrors), chests of drawers and sideboards all allow ample storage space. The kitchen furniture includes a sturdy table and kitchen cabinet and three types of chairs. Chair-beds, bed-settees, book shelves, an occasional table and nursery furniture are also included in the exhibition."

The Lord Mayor said that "As fashions in period furniture changed, purchasers of utility furniture might have pieces which one day would be regarded as a rare type of 1943." Even though the pieces were made "on austerity lines with a minimum of embellishment" the high quality of the utility furniture was noted, and that most of it was made locally. Although people could look at the furniture on show, Mr. Clifford King, the organiser of the exhibition, explained that it was not instantly available in the shops, as "the retailer cannot buy utility furniture to stock, but merely to meet orders." In fact a permit was necessary to buy furniture and these were only granted "where a necessity to purchase could be proved." Applications to buy had to go to the Fuel Overseer, and hire purchase terms were available. The chairman of the Chamber of Commerce Retail Committee Roland C. Larking [a Norwich accountant] thanked the Lord Mayor and members of the Women's Voluntary Service who staffed the exhibition.

From the 26th June for two weeks there was an intensive drive to collect books and waste paper. Arthur Cleveland as Lord Mayor, with H. E. Upcher, Chairman of Norfolk County Council, wrote a letter to the *Eastern Daily Press* saying "A tremendous salvage effort is being organised throughout the county with the object of collecting one million books, magazines and periodicals for reading matter for all branches of the services, restocking blitzed libraries, and for the hospitals. The balance, unsuitable for any of the above, will be used for repulping for munitions."

Unfortunately not as many books as had been hoped for were donated during the two weeks, and the appeal was extended by another seven days and the target reduced to a quarter of a million. The press reported that "The first Norwich child to obtain a field marshal's badge for collecting 250 books is Lewis Williamson of 106 Connaught Road, and the Lord Mayor has sent an appropriate letter."

The Lady Mayoress, Evelyn Cleveland, wrote on 26th June concerning another of her interests. "The voting papers for the forthcoming election of candidates for the Royal Eastern Counties Institution for the Mentally Defective are now in the hands of the subscribers. Will the subscribers kindly sign and then send these papers, with the list of candidates, unmarked, to the Hon. Secretary of the Norwich Ladies Association, Mrs. S. H. L. Moyle, J.P, 13 Christchurch Road, who will allot them to the most urgent Norwich case."

The work of a Lord Mayor was busy and varied. In June Dr. Cleveland received a letter from Mr. Alexander Dodman of Paisley looking for relatives, who he believed were blacksmiths in the city. He wrote "My grandfather was the son of a blacksmith who went to sea and became a captain of a small sailing vessel. His wife was named Chambling and they had a fairly large family. They scattered, one son to Yorkshire, farming, and a sister married an hotel keeper in Norwich called Kett's Castle [a pub at 29 Ketts Hill]. A brother joined the Royal Artillery and took his discharge in Bangalore, India, where I met him in 1898. I met his son in Rangoon when I was on the Indian staff in 1900. This son, my cousin, was then a bandsman in the West Riding Regiment. My father's parents dying, he was brought up by an aunt who lived in White Hart Street, Aylsham. She died about 1900."

Alexander Dodman went on to say that his father joined the Royal Nottinghamshire Regiment and saw service in the Kaffir campaigns. "Born in the regiment in 1873, I followed my father's footsteps, served in the last war, retiring as a sergeant-major. I would like to get in touch with any relatives, especially of the cousin I met in Rangoon." How the Lord Mayor tried to find out for Mr. Dodman, and whether he succeeded, is not recorded.

On 3rd July the Lord Mayor opened the new Citizens Advice Bureau on the ground floor of the City Hall. He said the bureau was one of those things which, once started, one wondered why it had not been provided before. Miss Clarkson, Chairman of the City Council's Social Committee which recommended setting up the bureau, described it as a place where anyone could ask any question, put forward any problem that was causing a worry, with every hopeful expectation of getting an answer on the spot. The full time secretary was a Miss Green who was said to have considerable experience in social work. Being in the City Hall meant that any query that could not be dealt with by Miss Green, could hopefully be answered by the Town Clerk, Bernard Storey, or any other department within the building. The Lord Mayor said it was a very good and sound venture that he was sure would bring excellent results. Before this any social welfare questions were dealt with at the Central and branch libraries by those libraries' staff.

The Lord Mayor and E. W. Woodhead, as President and Chairman respectively of the Local Air Training Corps, wrote an open letter to the *Eastern Daily Press* asking for donations. The letter, which appeared in the paper on 9th July, said "The normal expenses of the ATC are met from public funds, but money required for recreational facilities, in addition to that found by the cadets, can only come by public appeal. The local committee now desire to raise the sum of £300 for the general welfare of the cadets, primarily, if possible, to purchase band instruments.

"Members of the ATC are trained mainly for service in the RAF, and freely give their time after working hours. We feel their efforts should be recognised, and therefore make this appeal to the citizens of Norwich."

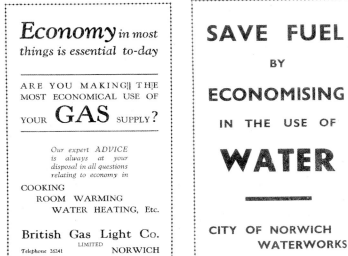

The Bishops Palace in Norwich, on the north side of the Cathedral, was officially opened on Saturday July 12th as an American Red Cross Services Club for the use of American troops visiting Norwich when on leave. The American flag and the Union flag were displayed together as a band from the Royal Norfolk Regiment played British and American melodies. There were speeches in the oak panelled room, and the Bishop of Norwich, Dr. Percy Herbert, handed over "a massive old key of the Palace to Lt. Col. Fiearing, representing Brig Gen. J. S. Hodges, U.S.A.A.F. From the officer the key was passed to Pte. Harry Goldstein, chairman of the soldiers' committee of the club, who declared: 'If only our folks and friends back home knew how well we are being taken care of they would be relieved of worry'".

The Bishop said "The use to which the Palace was being put was somewhat remarkable, when one thought of the long history and the many occupiers of the house, the foundations, at least, of which were as old as the cathedral." The Lord Mayor, in a welcome to the Americans, said "the ground on which the club stood was peculiarly reminiscent of the ancient past of Norwich, and to us was hallowed ground. It is most fitting that I, the present holder of an ancient office, whose roll of past holders extends back for more than 500 years, should welcome you to a building offered by him who is a direct official descendant of that first Bishop of Norwich, who founded our great cathedral." Mr. Robert Bondie, the chief administrator of A.R.C. [American Red Cross] Services to American Armed Forces said that "the hope that through the A.R.C., the medium which spoke for the heart of America, there would be a binding together of the hearts of American men and women with their friends and cousins here."

Raising money for various causes, as we have seen, continued, with much willingness all round. On the evening of Thursday 15th July the Norfolk and Norwich Comrades Club, at a ceremony on the stage of the Regent cinema in Prince of Wales Road, handed over a cheque of £235 to the Lord Mayor towards the Prisoners of War Fund. There was a competition as well, of which the prize winners handed back their prizes to the donors – another example of generosity.

The Newmarket Road Sports Ground [now Town Close School playing field on the corner of Daniels Road] was host to the National Fire Service No. 13 Fire Force Area competitions on Sunday 18th July. These consisted of units from the whole of Norfolk, Suffolk and parts of Cambridgeshire. Tasks tackled were three-man stirrup pump drill, light trailer pump drill, six-men heavy unit drill, one-man hydrant drill, four-men hydrant drill, five-men large trailer pump drill, three-men ladder drill and Officers large trailer pump drill.

There was also women's squad drill, women's stirrup pump drill, five women light trailer pump drills and messenger's relay races. Officers of the National Fire Service acted as stewards, judges and time keepers. The competitions were interspersed with physical training displays by men and women, march-pasts by the Messenger Services and the Dispatch Rider Services. The band of the Royal Norfolk Regiment played incidental music.

Alexandra Rose Day

Sir—The Alexandra Rose Day collection will take place in the city on Saturday next, the 15th inst. Similar collections will be made in the county on or near the same date. Last year the collection was a record and for the first time exceeded £1000.

I earnestly appeal to the citizens to assist me in this effort by subscribing generously so that the Norfolk and Norwich and Jenny Lind Hospitals and the Norfolk and Norwich Eye Infirmary, which are in urgent need of funds, may receive help to carry on their excellent work. The whole of this collection is carried out by voluntary helpers, and the only costs are for postage, printing and stationery which usually amount to about £3 or £4.

So many of the younger generation have joined the various Services or are engaged on war work of national importance that I wish to appeal this year particularly to the older ladies and gentlemen to come forward and assist on the day of the collection. Those willing to help should send in their names and addresses and the district in which they would prefer to help to the hon. organisers, Alexandra Rose Day Collection, 38, St. Giles Norwich, or report at one of the depots on the day of the collection —Yours very truly.

EVELYN M. CLEVELAND,
Lady Mayoress.

The Lady Mayoress, Evelyn Cleveland, wrote to the Eastern Daily Press *about the Alexandra Rose Day of June 15th.*

The majority of the competitions were won by A Division, which covered Norwich, North Norfolk, Wymondham and Forehoe and Henstead [combined Rural District Council area]. Prizes were presented to the winning teams and individuals by Major General A. C. Fuller, Deputy Regional Commissioner. The Lord Mayor and Lady Mayoress, and Alderman H. E. Witard watched the competitions.

The Messenger Service mentioned was open to any male between the ages of sixteen and eighteen who could be trusted to take messages quickly and securely to and from the police, ARP, Fire Service etc., either on foot or bicycle, particularly when telephone wires were down and roads blocked.

The Lord Mayor and party visited the Old Meeting House Congregational Church in Colegate on Sunday 25th July 1943 as part of the tercentenary celebrations of the organisation.

The Old Meeting House Congregational Church in Colegate was founded in 1643, and 300 years later, in 1943, they celebrated their tercentenary. The present building was not erected until 1693, being an example of free church architecture of the time, as well as one of the first congregational churches in the country. On Sunday 25th July they celebrated in style, with the Lord Mayor and Corporation party in full regalia, along with four members of Parliament visiting the church. The Rev. W. Ellis Pearson, Moderator of the Eastern Division, conducted the morning service, and the minister Rev. P. J. Lawton welcomed the distinguished visitors. The collection taken went to the Norfolk and Norwich Hospital.

The *Eastern Evening News* was always quick at reporting what happened earlier in the day, and an example of this was on 27th July when funds raised by the Alexandra Rose Day totalling £1,361.10s were handed out at a meeting in the Guildhall during the morning. Presided over by the Lady Mayoress, amongst the recipients were the Jenny Lind Hospital getting £185, and the Norfolk and Norwich Eye Infirmary getting £56.10s. The main beneficiary was the Norfolk and Norwich Hospital which received £1000. 1943 was a record year for the fund raising, breaking all previous

Alexandra Rose Day records - all this through the sale of roses. At the meeting Mrs. Cleveland and Mrs. Brooksbank were nominated as life governors of the hospital.

On Friday 30th July in the morning the Lord Mayor presided over a public meeting at the Hippodrome Theatre along with Field Marshall Sir Philip Chetwode, chairman of the headquarters of the British Red Cross and Order of St. John. Sir Philip said "We have never been asked for anything by the three Services, all over the world, from Hong Kong to the West Indies, and from Iceland to Cape Town, that we have not been able to provide. Our funds now total £23,000,000 and the penny-a-week and rural pennies scheme brings in £100,000 a week." He talked about the heavy losses of material through enemy action earlier in the war, and explained that "home activities included 232 convalescent homes and hospitals, 22 residential nurseries for young children, numerous first aid posts and rest centres, 111 stores posts at selected points, 1,120 ambulances, mobile X-ray units, canteen vans and field kitchens, and a department where relatives could inquire about missing and wounded men anywhere in the world. Abroad they had set up convalescent homes, depots of stores wherever needed, a foreign relations department concerning occupied and enemy countries, a postal message scheme to place people isolated on the Continent in touch with relatives here, help for our allies, including £3,300,000 for Russia through Mrs. Churchill's scheme, and a big hospital in China, as well as for refugees from all over Europe who went to Spain."

The Field Marshall went on to describe the prisoner of war camps "as the funds heaviest commitment." He gave information as to the conditions in the 70 camps in Germany and the 44 in Italy. Sir Phillip concluded by appealing for the continued support of their work by the public, describing the work of the two organisations as "a debt of honour."

In the afternoon people were getting ready for the War Charities fund raising week which was to begin the next day. That Friday afternoon at Chamberlins [drapers and house furnishers] store on Guildhall Hill [Tesco now occupies the site] there was a "Spare a Trinket Competition". Opened by the Lord Mayor and Lady Mayoress, items on display included a black silk parasol used by Queen Victoria, a jade duck of the Ming Dynasty loaned by the Queen, a miniature picture of the Empress Josephine, and a gold brooch of the Canadian maple leaf loaned by Winston Churchill. At the close of the exhibition that day, £50 had been raised.

The War Charities Week proper began at 10.30 on the morning of Saturday 31st July when the "Lord Mayor started a train of pennies along Castle Meadow today" reported the *Eastern Evening News* in their afternoon edition. This was organised by the Girl Guides, and 'Miss Norwich', Eileen Votier, was in attendance along "with her ladies in waiting Miss Doreen Dufour and Miss Beryl Vickers." All three girls were aged sixteen. Miss Votier had been elected Miss Norwich by the audience at the Hippodrome Theatre on Monday 26th July. She was reported as being a student at Martin's Business College - which was situated at the Bank Plain end of London Street.

In the afternoon there was an auction of wines and spirits in the Corn Hall [in Exchange Street - now part of Jarrolds site] at 3 o'clock, and at the Grammar School a sale, folk dancing and music by the Yareside Dance Band. There was also a film show of documentaries - *In Enemy Hands* and *Believe it or Not* both showing the work of the Red Cross.

The fund raising got off to a good start. The 'Spare a Trinket sale' brought in £80, the line of pennies on Castle Meadow totalled £67.10s.9d, the wine and spirit auction at the Corn Hall raised £750, the sale and entertainment at the Grammar School raised £500. Over £4000 was raised on the Saturday.

The day ended with Miss Norwich appearing on stage at the Hippodrome, where "she was introduced to her public" as the *Eastern Daily Press* put it.

War Charities Week began in Norwich on Saturday 31st July 1943 at 10.30am with a line of coins. The Lord Mayor started with the first few pennies, then watches as 'Miss Norwich', Eileen Votier, adds her contribution to the line along Castle Meadow, not far from Opie Street. Standing behind Miss Norwich are her two ladies-in-waiting Miss Doreen Dufour and Miss Beryl Vickers.

On Sunday 1st August there was a drumhead review with representatives of the R.A.F., the Home Guard, the Women's Services, Sea Cadets, the National Fire Service, Civil Defence, St. John Ambulance Brigade, British Red Cross, Boy Scouts, Boys Brigade, St. John Cadets, Girl Guides, Girl Cadets and ex-service men's associations. They first paraded on the Cattle Market site [then a big open space now covered with the Castle Quarter] then in one long procession they went past Norwich City Hall to the sounds of music from the bands of the Army, the Home Guard, the Norwich Lads Club and Boys Brigades. The salute was taken by 'a high ranking' Army Officer, a Wing Commander from the R.A.F. and the Lord Mayor.

In the evening there was a concert in Chapel Field Gardens with the Reepham Junior Band, and a Brains Trust at the Hippodrome presided over by the Bishop of Norwich, where questions were asked and the Bishop gave 'amusing and brilliant replies'. A large audience listened to Major Bryan of the U.S.A.A.F. [United States Army Air Force] talking about Anglo-American relations and the coming together of the two; the Bishop of Norwich acting as Chairman followed this up suggesting an extension of the British Commonwealth of Nations, which Major Bryan did not agree with. One of the panel members, Miss C. Behrens, answered a question about what would be the trend in women's fashions after the war by saying "Shorter and tighter skirts in view of the shortage of materials." Mr. Bulman could not answer the question of why some men went bald!

'Whiffler' writing in the *Eastern Evening News* on Monday 2nd August said "I think I award the prize of the evening to the Lord Mayor for his prompt correct definition of the word 'wayzgoose' as a printers annual outing. I wonder how many of the others present would have thought it was 'a kind of wading bird'."

The 2nd of August was Bank Holiday Monday, with "a variety of entertainments which provided something to see and do from morning to night" reported the *Eastern Daily Press*. An exhibition of equipment used on fighters and bombers at the War Charities Centre in Rampant Horse Street "attracted one of the biggest crowds ever to visit the centre." There was a Merlin engine as used in the Spitfire, a self-sealing petrol tank as used in Beaufighters, a 20mm Hispano canon, a bomb sight "used in a recent Essen raid", a parachute outfit, emergency rations for bomber dinghies and oxygen breathing equipment.

There was a fun-fair in Chapel Field Gardens and at the "Orford Place static water basin all day long the public tried to sink a dinghy with pennies, a feature arranged by the N.F.S." This brought in over £9. The water tank was in the site of bombed out Curls store [now Debenhams is on the site between Rampant Horse Street and Orford Place]. In the evening there was "a novelty dance organised by 'C' Group Wardens", a Carnival Dance at the Y.W.C.A. and a White Wings Concert Party in Park Lane Lecture Hall with music, a puppet show and ventriloquist act by 17 year-old Gerald Morter.

By Tuesday 3rd of August the money raised so far during the War Charities Week had passed the half way mark of the hoped for £15,000. The fund raising schemes continued, and that Tuesday there was a dance at Ailwyn Hall organised by the 'Railwaymen's Social and Athletic Club', and a Whist Drive at Ashworth and Pike's [they had premises in Davey Place, St. Stephens, St. Benedict's and No.17 Earlham Road] who were bakers and confectioners. In the evening Miss Norwich, Eileen Votier, and the Lord Mayor attended a dance at the Lido [next to the Capitol cinema in the Aylsham Road and later called Norwood Rooms] organised by the U.S.A.A.F. There was a Hill Billy band and a swing band, and, said the local paper, 'a crowded house'. In fact there were 1,200 people at the Lido - "the biggest crowd ever to attend this amusement centre." £230 was raised.

A new Y.W.C.A. Hostel at 8-10 The Close was opened by the Bishop of Norwich on Wednesday 4th August. At this hostel there was accommodation

AIR TRAINING CORPS

The undermentioned Units will parade on **SUNDAY NEXT, AUGUST 8th, 1943**

at the

NORWICH CITY HALL

for inspection by

THE DIRECTOR OF THE AIR TRAINING CORPS (W. W. Wakefield, Esq., M.P.)

The Right Worshipful the Lord Mayor of Norwich will be present. All units will fall in on the City Hall Car Park at 14.30 hours. 230 (1st Norwich) Squadron, 231 (2nd Norwich), 232 (3rd Norwich), 233 (4th Norwich). 1132 (Stalham and Wroxham), 1496 (Blofield), 2102 (Acle)

Advance publicity for the 8th August.

for 44 women. The beds had quilted patchwork bedspreads which were donated from Canada via the W.V.S. The hostel had a sitting room, canteen, and laundry room. Field Marshall Lord Ironside spoke of the great part women were playing in the armed forces and how they had fitted into service life. Miss Charlotte Niven, national representative of the Y.W.C.A., gave an account of the war work done by the Association, and the Lord Mayor proposed a vote of thanks to the speakers.

Also on Wednesday the 4th the Lord Mayor sent a telegram to the Queen "offering the loyal and sincere greetings of the citizens of Norwich to Her Majesty on the occasion of her birthday."

Thursday August 5th saw thousands of boys and girls at a fete in support of War Charities Week in Boundary Park [off Boundary Road] organised by Group K of the A.R.P. and opened by John Brooksbank, Sheriff of Norwich. Miss Norwich, accompanied by her two ladies in waiting arrived in an open landau and "were cheered lustily by the young people" said the *Eastern Daily Press*. Miss Norwich gave a speech thanking the boys and girls and their parents for coming and hoped all would help reach the week's target, and even exceed it.

John Brooksbank said that the fete was not only for pleasure, but to make us think of "your older brothers abroad, and the great suffering which many of them might be undergoing; the sailors facing the dangers of the seas and thousands of others in order that children may be able to continue with their education and grow up into happy citizenship." The local paper's report said that "All afternoon the young people played at games, high-

Mrs Bunn of Caernarvon Road, Norwich, celebrated her 100th birthday with a visit from her son and daughter, and the Lord Mayor and Lady Mayoress on Wednesday 11th August 1943.

jumping, open races, stunt races, darts, football, swings and other games. There was a marionette show and a miniature railway contributed by R. E. Ward of New Costessey."

In the evening there was a War Charities Ball at the Samson and Hercules [opposite Erpingham Gate into the Cathedral] which brought in over £450, and the Group A Wardens held a dance at the Lido. Service personnel of the U.S.A.A.F. helped throughout the week, and on the Friday began organising flag day collections and a rodeo display show for the next day. In the evening there was another concert by the Park Lane Youth Centre this time at Sprowston Road Methodist Church.

On the Saturday, the 7th August, the flag day was in full swing. "From St. Stephens Gate to Thorpe Station, and the Cattle Market to Unthank Road, there will be about 28 selling centres, and hundreds of vendors will see to it that no part of the city will be left uncombed" reported the *Eastern Daily Press*. Organised by the British Red Cross Society and Order of St. John over £600 was raised. The rodeo show at Carrow Road football ground attracted 6000 people who watched "Galloping, leaping, lassoing their way about, and accompanied by the weird yodelling of 'Ragtime Annie' and 'Cowboy Sweetheart', aided by a Hill Billy Band, these American soldier-cowboys performed many feats of reckless but expert horsemanship."

Also that day there was a fete at the Recreation Road Ground [off Earlham Road] organised by G Group of the A.R.P. Wardens, and later Miss Norwich handed out prizes to winners of various competitions of the week. The day ended with bands playing, a boxing match, whist drives and dances. *The Eastern Daily Press* of Monday 9th could not report the exact figure raised during War Charities Week, but did say "Total last year exceeded."

On Sunday the 8th August the Lord Mayor was to have been at the City Hall to watch a march past by various local units of the A.T.C. cadets in company with William Wavell Wakefield, M.P. for Swindon and Director of the Air Training Corps. Dr. Cleveland is recorded as being 'indisposed', and his place taken by the Sheriff, John Brooksbank. From the City Hall steps Mr. Wakefield addressed the squadrons saying "The side with the best trained reserves will win the battle, and it was the job of the A.T.C. to see the Fleet Air Arm and the R.A.F. had such reserves. The A.T.C. had a great responsibility and were fulfilling it well. The opinion of Air Force officers was that our A.T.C. lads were responsible for higher standards when they entered the Forces, and recalled that in North Africa the Italian air force first, and afterwards the Luftwaffe, were forced from the skies by the determination of ground staffs, in serving the members of the air crews better than could the enemy. Airmen of the last war lost many comrades because they had to use obsolete machines or were not properly trained. The A.T.C. could go forward confident of doing a vital job, confident of having the best planes in the world to fly and service, and confident of being efficiently trained."

On the morning of Wednesday August 11th the Lord Mayor and Lady Mayoress visited Mrs. Sophia Jane Bunn in her home at 102 Caernarvon Road [between Earlham Road towards Avenue Road], Norwich. Mrs. Bunn was celebrating her 100th birthday, and had just received a telegram from the King and Queen.

Mrs. Bunn, the daughter of William Bailey, a builder, was born in West Pottergate and had spent most of her life in the city. She was married on 1st August 1867 at St. Bartholomew church, Heigham, to Robert Bunn, a surveyor. They had seven children "three of whom are alive" as the *Eastern Evening News* put it, and there were eight grandchildren and fourteen great-grandchildren. Although slightly deaf, she could read and write without the aid of glasses, and still did a little crocheting. She was not so mobile as she used to be, and had been carried to the air raid shelter when a raid was on, but now had a Morrison shelter which she slept in. Mrs. Cleveland presented Mrs. Bunn with a bouquet of carnations and roses. The report in the *Eastern Evening News* that evening said that Mrs. Bunn "was keenly interested in the Lord Mayor's chain of office. It was the first time she had seen it."

The Lord Mayor inspects National Fire Service [NFS] equipment on
the 18th August 1943 at the Fire Station which was in Bethel Street.

The Lord Mayor was at Norwich Fire Station in Bethel Street on the Wednesday 18th August to watch the National Fire Service men and women put on a display of their work and skills and show off the latest fire equipment. Dr. Cleveland with members of the Corporation watched as the men marched and drilled with "military precision" and the women, dressed in "white blouses and smart black shorts, their official physical training dress", gave a similar display.

The equipment included a demonstration of a pair of 100ft high turntable ladders with a fireman at the top of each. These machines cost £5,000 each.

There were rescues from the stations tower [in the courtyard at the back of the Fire Station] and a smoke filled room where the men wore breathing apparatus, and in Chapel Field Gardens a demonstration of accessing a water supply and pumping it through 600 feet of hose. The Lord Mayor watched all this with great interest and said, as a doctor, that "a well trained mind and well trained body went together. After the war they would look back on this service with a great deal of affection, because there was no comradeship like that between those who faced danger together." The displays and demonstrations marked the second anniversary of the National Fire Service.

While that was going on Mrs. Cleveland presided over a meeting of the Y.M.C.A. in St Giles [Nos. 48-50] celebrating the expansion and work of the organisation. Mr. G. F. Hubbard, the Area Secretary of the Y.M.C.A. said that there were now 28 centres in Norfolk compared with 6 at the beginning of the war. "Over 25,000 men had been given sleeping accommodation in the six-month period ending in March, and more than 300,000 meals were served in that period. Charges made to service men were fixed by service departments, and were in line with similar organisations such as the N.A.A.F.I. [Navy, Army & Air Force Institutes]. The charge for bed and breakfast, for example, including clean sheets, was between 1s and 1s 9d."

Friday 20th August the Lord Mayor oversaw a special Court of Freemen to admit Arthur Stanley Bird of 84 Wodehouse Street [between Spencer Street and Silver Road] who was employed as a chemist at the Electricity Power Station [by the River Wensum at Trowse]. His father, Ernest Bird, was also a Freeman who had been admitted in 1911, the honour being hereditary. Soon after the event, Arthur Bird was called up.

The Lady Mayoress and her daughter, Deenie Cleveland, attended a funeral service in the cathedral on Tuesday 24th August for Mrs. Sheepshanks, widow of a former Bishop of Norwich John Sheepshanks who had been Bishop between 1893 and 1910. They had married in 1870 and had 17 children. He died in 1912, so Mrs. Sheepshanks had been a widow for 31 years.

The Lord Mayor was to present a bronze medal - but as it was not ready at the time so a ribbon and certificate was presented temporarily - on behalf of the R.S.P.C.A. on Saturday 28th August to Inspector John McClusky for rescuing a horse from a dyke at Whitlingham marshes. "The horse had been trapped in the mud with just its head, neck and a part of its back visible. Inspector McClusky, at risk of great personal danger, crawled along two planks laid on the mud and reached the horse with a rope. Another horse then pulled on to the rope" said the Lord Mayor. The horse was rescued none the worse for its ordeal.

A few days later, on Wednesday 1st September, the Lord Mayor was at the riverside by the Grammar School playing fields between Pull's Ferry and Bishop Bridge, and about to board the *Lord Nelson*, the Sea Cadets training ship, when he recognised the craft as once being the paddle steamer *PS Lymington* which ran between the mainland and the Isle of White, for it was the very boat that he and his wife Evelyn Cleveland went on during their honeymoon in 1900. Once on board, the Lord Mayor, along with the

Part of the Belgium War Exhibition at the Castle Museum opened on Saturday 4th September 1943 by Mr. Auguste B. De Schrijver, the Belgian Minister of Economic Affairs. "The exhibits typify the stout resistance of the Belgian people at home, the part they are playing in the war effort over here, and the contribution of Belgium's great colony in the Congo to the resources of the United Nations,"

Inspecting Officer for the Eastern Area Lieutenant Commander Oates of the R.N.V.R. [Royal Naval Volunteer Reserve] and the Commanding Officer Lieutenant B. L. Misselbrook, cadets were lined up and inspected and decreed 'A Fine Parade'. "The corps has made excellent progress since it came under the direction of the Admiralty, and is recognised as a pre-entry training unit for the Naval Services" said the *Eastern Daily Press*.

Mr. Auguste B. De Schrijver, the Belgian Minister of Economic Affairs, was in Norwich on Saturday 4th September to open an exhibition at the Castle Museum showing the part Belgium and the Belgian Congo played in the war. He was accompanied by General Van Strydonck de Burkel, Inspector General of Belgian Forces. Mr. De Schrijver gave an opening speech saying "The Anglo friendship was a reality because it had been cemented with the blood of the soldiers of the two countries. Twice in a quarter of a century had Belgium known all the horrors of war; twice also had Belgian refugees found a hearty welcome in England."

Covering seven rooms in the Museum, the exhibition presented a variety of topics, including the invasion of Belgium, the capitulation on 28th May 1940, as well as maps, documents and photographs which illustrated the destruction of Tournai and other towns. The exhibition also contained reference to the execution of Nurse Edith Cavell in the previous war. A write up in the *Eastern Daily Press* said "The minister, Mr. Schrijver, declared 'We fight for the same political and moral aims. Britain and Belgium both believe in moral values, individual liberty, respect for the given word, true social progress and the free expression of religion.

"The spirit of freedom and resistance is more alive than ever and proof of it will be given when your troops enter Belgium as an army of liberation'. A vote of thanks to the Minister was accorded after speeches by the Sheriff (Mr. J. Brooksbank) and Mr. R. H. Mottram. The Lord Mayor and Alderman W. A. Riley expressed the thanks of the citizens to the Belgian Government for sending the exhibition to Norwich; and Sir Thomas Cook [M.P. for North Norfolk] thanked the Lord Mayor for presiding."

Mr. Auguste B. De Schrijver, the Belgian Minister of Economic Affairs has just laid a wreath at Nurse Edith Cavell's grave on Life's Green, on the south side of Norwich Cathedral. He is seen here looking away, on the Lord Mayor's right. In front of Schrijver to the left is General Van de Burkel.

Thursday 9th September was another busy day for the Lord Mayor, Lady Mayoress, officials, and the people of Norwich. The Acting Chief Commissioner of the St. John Ambulance Brigade, General Sir Clive Liddell, and Superintendent-in-Chief Lady Louis Mountbatten, arrived in the city along with other county Brigade officials, to attend a reception given by the Lord Mayor and Lady Mayoress at the City Hall, where an official photograph was taken. Then they went to the Royal Hotel for lunch where they were joined by the Lord Lieutenant Russell Colman. At 2.50pm Lady Mountbatten and the party went to St Andrews Hall to the Services Club sick bay jointly run by the St. John Ambulance Brigade and the Red Cross. Then they went to the Services Club canteen at Thorpe Station, and onto an unnamed convalescent hospital similarly jointly staffed. Later they went to the Samson and Hercules on Tombland where they had tea and met the cadets, ambulance and nursing staff of both organisations. After that they went to the Grammar School playing field in the Lower Close where about one thousand members of the St. John Ambulance Nursing and Cadet

Thursday 9th September 1943. The official photograph, taken on the City Hall steps of the visit of General Sir Clive Liddel, Acting Chief Commissioner of the St. John Ambulance Brigade, and Lady Louis Mountbatten, Superintendent-in-Chief. Also in the picture are Norwich and county officials. Front row left to right – Evelyn Cleveland, the Lady Mayoress; General Sir Clive Liddel; Dr. Arthur Cleveland, the Lord Mayor; Lady Mountbatten; Lady Albemarle [believed to be]; John Brooksbank, the Sheriff; and Mrs. Brooksbank.

divisions from across the county, including Norwich, put on a "spectacular parade". Sir Clive Liddell took the salute and presented Lady Albemarle with a special badge in recognition of her appointment as County Vice-President of the Cadet Corps. Lady Mountbatten gave a speech saying amongst other things, "How pleased she was to see the large number of cadets who would in future assist in the reconstruction overseas and at home."

It was not only ceremonial events the Lord Mayor had to attend - there were letters to write and correspondence to deal with as we have seen. In the second week of September he received a letter from the father of a soldier stationed in Norwich praising the way the city was looking after servicemen through the various service clubs. "We have never had a dull letter from him" the father wrote, adding "My wife and I thought it is so nice to have the feeling that, although the family is being broken up due to the war, they were still being looked after so well and not just wandering around at a loose end. So please accept this letter as just a small appreciation of what is being done, not only for our son, but thousands of others as well, and they all would join us in saying thank you Norwich, we shall never forget what you have done." What the Lord Mayor said in his reply we may never know, as it appears not to have survived.

At a gathering of Norwich Savings Group secretaries in the Stuart Hall on 15th September, the Lord Mayor congratulated them on their work saying

"You have done a double duty. You have helped the country at a time when it needs all the help it can get and you have persuaded people to help themselves." This was all about the raising of funds through the various savings weeks including Wings For Victory. Herbert Gowen, Chairman of the Executive Committee, comparing the report for the past year with that of the last report made on a peace-time basis in 1938, he pointed out that "that there were now 235 groups, as compared with 42, membership of 12,436, as compared with 731, and a total amount saved of £110,122, as against £3,251. The total amount saved by commercial and industrial groups since the commencement of the War Savings campaign was £320,896." For those groups who exceeded their targets during the Wings For Victory week the Lord Mayor presented certificates of honour.

The Norwich Civil Defence Messenger Service held their sports meeting at the Newmarket Road ground during the afternoon of Saturday 18th September. Competitors included those from the National Fire Service and the County Messenger Service. The Lord Mayor presented prizes. According to the report "S/L Bushell of the Norwich Service won the 100 yards, 220 yards, 440 yards, and ran a lap of the relay race."

Photographs of damaged churches in Norwich and Norfolk were amongst the displays in St. Giles Parish Hall on Cow Hill on Thursday 23rd September. It was opened by the Lord Mayor. The report in the *Eastern Daily Press* said "The series of photographs depicting the fact that the church collectively, is fully alive to the religious problems brought about by the war, includes some realistic photographs lent by the Ministry of Information showing the Nazi attitude towards religion and religious objects." The report in the *Eastern Evening News* added "Two particularly striking examples show the Nazis taking part in a mock procession of the Blessed Sacrament and masquerading in vestments stolen from a Polish church."

The idea for the exhibition, which included religious films shown throughout the three days it was on, came from the churchwarden of St. Giles, Mr. W. D. Varney. There was no charge, though there were collecting boxes at the doors in aid of the Norfolk War Charities Fund.

The Bishop of Norwich, Dr. Percy Herbert, as president of the Norwich Institution for the Blind, was due to chair a meeting on 23rd September but was unwell, so the Lord Mayor had to step in and preside. Mr. C.R.A. Hammond of the Committee of Management recalled "The difficulties which ensued through the bombing of the premises [in Magdalen Street] the first thing to do after the war would be to erect new workshops in order to move workers back into comfortable buildings. At the same time move the old people back into their home. They were being extremely well treated by Yarmouth, but they looked on Norwich as their home."

Saturday 25th September. The Lord Mayor chaired a meeting at the Stuart Hall where the Regional Commissioner for the Eastern Region National Savings Movement Wings For Victory campaign, Mr. K. Wilson, said that £30,182 had been raised across the area. This "was an increase of 20.7 percent over the figure for Warship Week. This was a wonderful achievement, the percentage increase being double that for the country."

TANKS FOR ATTACK

Norwich

Your little extra!

—will help a lot

Norwich aims at sending
10 CHURCHILLS into the attack

INCREASE YOUR SAVINGS TO-DAY

SPACE KINDLY PRESENTED TO THE NORWICH SAVINGS COMMITTEE BY
WALLACE KING, LTD.

The house furnishers Wallace King Ltd. of 24-26 Prince of Wales Road paid for this appeal space in the Eastern Daily Press.

The Lord Mayor, who had welcomed all the delegates, said "The movement and the work they were doing were of the greatest national importance. When the war was over this country would have an extraordinary difficult task ahead of it. Just as it had been the mainstay of democracy in Europe in war, so it would have to be in peace. One of the first essentials for that was a sound economic and financial policy. This required that people should practise thrift." At the meeting a resolution was passed calling on the National Committee to quickly formulate and announce plans for post-war Britain.

The next day, Sunday the 26th September, was Battle of Britain Sunday, and there were parades of the fighting Services and Civil Defence, and special church services throughout the county. In Norwich, at 11.0 o'clock, the Lord Mayor, Deputy Lord Mayor, the Sheriff and civic heads and officials attended a special service at the Cathedral. There were also representatives from the Royal Air Force, Ack-Ack [home front anti-aircraft guns] Command, Women's Auxiliary Air Force, Auxiliary Territorial

Service, Royal Observer Corps, Home Guard, Civil Defence and Norwich City Police. The sermon was given by the Dean Dr. H. S. Cranage. He called for preparation for the future, and "to meet the needs of our men in de-mobilisation."

After the service there was a collection by RAF flying crews and members of the WAAF for the RAF Benevolent Fund. £37. 9s. 9d. was raised. At the Carlton cinema on All Saints Green there was a special service for men and women of the Wardens Service. Mr. A. Gibbs played the organ and led the singing of hymns - the words to which were shown on the screen. £15 10s was raised for the RAF Benevolent Fund.

Earlier in the year, on the 18th April, we heard of a small girl, Brenda Cozens, rescued from the River Wensum. A similar thing happened approximately five weeks later on Saturday 29th May when on hearing screams 46 year-old William Webster, a brewer's storeman at Whitbread Ltd. bottled beer stores in King Street, ran out to find a boy struggling in the middle of the river. Webster jumped in and swam to the 4½ year-old boy - Michael Blyth of 144 King Street. The report stated that "He held him up and commenced to swim back when the heavy apron he was wearing got round his legs and put him in difficulties. When near the bank a railwayman threw a rope to him and assisted them out."

This was not the only rescue from the Wensum that year. On Wednesday 23rd June Terence Oldman, an 18 year-old coal porter at Thomas Moy Ltd., was riding in a lorry in King Street when a man stopped the lorry to say a child was in the river. The three-year-old - Raymond Withey of 8 Stuart Road [off King Street near Carrow Road bridge], was about 10 feet out in the river. "Without hesitation Oldman jumped in, swam to the child and brought him to the bank where he was helped out by an onlooker."

At the Guildhall in Norwich on Wednesday 29th September the Lord Mayor presented both these rescuers - William Webster and Terence Oldman - with the Royal Humane Society's certificates for their actions. "It would have been a tragedy if these two brave men had lost their lives through the misbehaviour of these children. No doubt the Chief Constable had taken note of the incidents. Both acts showed great presence of mind and great bravery" said the Lord Mayor.

In Elm Hill at this time there was a Club where commissioned officers of the Forces could meet, relax and enjoy club life and the usual recreations while staying in Norwich. But the need arose for additional and quieter premises for those on short stays in the city. A committee, led by the Lord Mayor, set about organising such a venue. Mrs. Geoffrey Colman, whose husband had died in 1935, was also very keen on the idea, and generously leased from the Dean and Chapter an empty house in the Lower Close - No. 32 in fact, just two doors away from where Arthur Cleveland lived - and offered it to the committee. They then set about making it a homely place for officers to stay in for up to two nights. Wallace King, described as Home Furnishers in Prince of Wales Road, gave some carpets and the Colman sisters loaned furniture. There were rest rooms, sleeping accommodation and a bar. The committee was able to carry out the necessary alterations with the aid of a substantial contribution from the

WOMEN WANTED

for work of national importance in Canteens serving the Forces in the Eastern Counties.

COUNTER ASSISTANTS

GENERAL ASSISTANTS

KITCHENMAIDS

STOREWOMEN

Good wages are paid and attractive uniforms provided free. The work should appeal to all women not engaged on essential duties, especially those classified as "immobile." Write or apply personally for pamphlet and full information to:—

NAVY, ARMY AND AIR FORCE INSTITUTES
(Dept. C 77)

14, Bank Street, Norwich

Local interview arranged

From 29th January 1943 all women between the ages of 18 and 45 were required to offer themselves for either part time or full time work as an alternative to joining the Services. Factory work, nursing etc. were suggested. Only women solely looking after children under 14 were exempt.

Norfolk War Charities Fund. A cook and steward were employed, along with Mr. Arnold Kent as secretary.

Officers from all three fighting services met the Lord Mayor and the committee at an informal reception at the new Club on Monday 4ᵗʰ October. "Further financial support came from the Director General of Army Welfare and the Eastern Command Welfare Officer, and the organisers have had the whole-hearted co-operation of senior officers of all three branches of the fighting services, as well as of the W.R.N.S. [Women's Royal Naval Service], the A.T.S. [Women's Auxiliary Territorial Service] and the W.A.A.F. [Women's Auxiliary Air Force]. Women officers of the Services will have the advantage of membership, although facilities for overnight stays are available only for men" said a report in the *Eastern Daily Press*.

There were some disagreements at the Norwich City Council meeting on Tuesday 5ᵗʰ of October when a Ministry of Health report about the city contained a paragraph which council members objected to. Mr. F. C. Jex [Alderman and Deputy Lord Mayor] said "From the report one got an intelligent and interesting picture of the health of the citizens." But as chairman of the Education Committee he went on to say that he must "emphatically protest against some of the nonsense it contained."

The author of the report, Dr. Soothill, wrote "Reference to the vital statistics shows that the number of known illegitimate births has increased materially, and I have had reports that even a few married women are being somewhat more promiscuous than usual. This is not surprising in view of the agencies at work tending to break up family and home life, such as the employment of women, nursery schools and classes, and communal feeding."

Mr. Jex said "This is the strangest statement I have ever read. It does not say that the standard of morality among a greater number of women is becoming lower, but that the people regularly doing this sort of thing are increasing the number of occasions on which their moral character is in question. The M.O.H. gives three reasons for it, two of which, nursery schools and communal feeding, represent national policy and the policy of this council, two very desirable aspects of organised communal life. He asks you to accept the fact that because you administer nursery schools and communal feeding you are encouraging and producing the opportunity for a much lower standard of morality. I take grave exception to the M.O.H. publishing this in our name, a report that will circulate throughout the country, without giving us the chance to prove it is unjustified." Mr. Jex urged the council to disapprove of this paragraph in the report.

Councillor H. W. Palmer seconded it saying "The M.O.H. had expressed his opinion, as he had a right to do, but it was likely to be regarded as the opinion of the council and there was no evidence to support the suggestion that promiscuity among married women arose from nursery schools or communal feeding. The M.O.H. has made the mistake of looking at secondary causes, instead of the primary cause. War was the greatest immorality that could occur in human beings."

Alderman H. E. Witard suggested "that the report should be referred back to the committee for the comment complained of to be deleted." There were further suggestions, both for and against. Mr. H. Jarrold said he thought "the Council would have been wise to follow the action of the

Health Committee, receive the report, but make it clear that it disassociated itself from the views of the doctor on this point." By 28 votes to 8 the Council adopted Mr. Jex's proposal that the council 'should express strong disapproval of the paragraph in question'. The council also accepted Mr. Jex's suggestion that printed slips giving information on the subject should be given out with each copy of the report.

FAMOUS PICTURES FOR NORWICH

MR. COLMAN TO BEQUEATH CROWN POINT COLLECTION

PROVISION FOR A GALLERY

The Lord Mayor (Dr. A. J. Cleveland) told a meeting of Norwich City Council, over which he presided yesterday, that Mr. Colman had intimated his intention to bequeath to the city his collection of pictures and drawings by artists of the Norwich School.

The Lord Mayor said Mr. Colman

"Mr. Colman's gift to the city of Norwich of his collection of pictures and drawings of the Norwich School is the greatest benefaction of British paintings since Turner bequeathed the contents of his gallery to the nation" said Paul Oppe, a former Director of the Victoria and Albert Museum on hearing the Lord Mayor's announcement of Russell Colman's generosity at the Norwich City Council meeting on 5th October 1943.

At that meeting on Tuesday 5th of October 1943, the Lord Mayor gave out the information that Russell Colman was to bequeath his collection of pictures and drawings by artists of the Norwich School to the city. Colman had written "I desire to offer my collection as a whole to the Corporation of Norwich in token of my affection for the city of my birth, and in acknowledgement of the honour and the unfailing courtesy and kindness I have received from my fellow citizens."

The collection was begun by James Jeremiah Colman in the 1860s with examples of John and William Crome, John Sell Cotman, George Vincent, James Stark, Joseph and Alfred Stannard and many others. J. J. Colman had already bequeathed many of these pictures to the Castle Museum upon his death in 1898. His son, Russell James Colman added to the collection over the years, and had many water-colours and oils restored in the 1930s.

Russell Colman also wrote in his letter to the Lord Mayor "I realise that on account of the size and composition of my collection a special gallery, or preferably a sequence of rooms, will be needed, and I have therefore empowered my trustees in my will to find the necessary funds - up to a specified figure - for the erection and equipment for such a building." The collection consisted of 228 oil paintings and 985 water-colours.

Dr. Cleveland said at the council meeting "The big industrial firm bearing the name of Colman has long been an asset of great value to the city. It gives, and has given employment to many thousands of our citizens, and if the great success it has achieved has brought riches to its owners, all of us must agree that they have never failed to show that they fully appreciate that the advantages wealth gives carry with them obligations. For several generations the men and women of the Colman family have given in full measure of their money and their service to this city, and this gift is a fitting culmination of the many and varied public services rendered by the present Lord Lieutenant of the county. It is very appropriate that a collection of pictures should form a lasting memorial to one who in addition to many public activities has been a generous patron and connoisseur of art."

Russell Colman was Lord Lieutenant of Norfolk (the Monarchs representative) from 1929 to 1944. Here photographed in 1943.

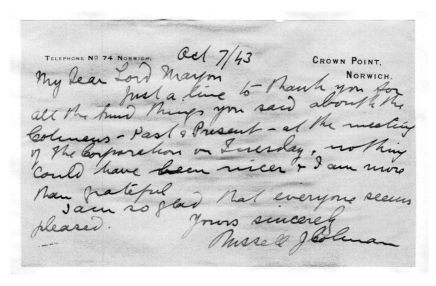

TELEPHONE Nº 74 NORWICH.

Oct 7/43

CROWN POINT,
NORWICH.

Russell Colman's note to the Lord Mayor after the announcement that the Colman collection of paintings and drawings was to be bequeathed to the City of Norwich.

Russell Colman wrote to the Lord Mayor on 7th October saying "Just a line to thank you for all the kind things you said about the Colmans - past and present – at the meeting of the Corporation on Tuesday, nothing could have been nicer and I am more than grateful. I am so glad that everyone seems pleased."

Russell Colman, who lived at Crown Point, just outside the city, died in 1946 and his wishes were carried out, with the formal opening of the newly constructed galleries taking place in June 1951. Today visitors can wander round the Colman Art Galleries and see some of the wonderful works of the Norwich School artists.

There was an air raid on Norwich during the evening of Thursday 7th October which caused little damage apart from making a 30ft deep crater near the railway lines at Lakenham, temporally halting trains on the double track line. No one was hurt.

Mr. Olav Hindahl, the Norwegian Minster of Commerce, spent the weekend of the 9th and 10th of October in Norwich as the guest of the Lord Mayor and Lady Mayoress. Mr. Hindahl was in Norwich to open the Norwegian Exhibition in the Castle Museum. In the Art Gallery the Lord Mayor spoke of "Norway's stirring maritime history reminding the gathering that Europe and, indeed, many countries of the world, had received a deep and lasting influence from those men who sailed from Norway's rugged coasts. He had been told on excellent authority, he said, that in none of the occupied countries had the Germans met with such heart-breaking and stolid resistance as from the men, women and children of Norway" reported the *Eastern Daily Press*.

The Norwegian Exhibition in the Castle Museum opened on Saturday 9th October 1943. In the picture are Mr. Olav Hindahl, Minister of Commerce, Arthur Cleveland looking through his monocle at an exhibit, and Sir Thomas Cook, MP for North Norfolk.

The Norwegian exhibition in the Castle Museum.

Mr. Hindahl spoke of "This lovely and ancient city, and personal contact with Norfolk people, was a happy occasion, because of the Norwegian Royal Family's association with the county. He recalled that Queen Maud spent a great deal of her time at Appleton House [the house, near Flitcham, was demolished in 1984] and a further link with Norfolk, which Norwegians cherished, was the fact that their future King, Crown Prince Olav, was born at Appleton House. 'We can almost claim to have a Norfolk man as heir to the Norwegian throne' he added amid applause."

He went on "Telling of the part in the war of Norway's reconstituted forces, the Minister reminded the gathering that from April 1940, some 300 Norwegian ships had been sunk and about 2000 seaman had perished. Prior to the invasion they had already lost 54 ships, but, he said 'I think the battle of the seas has now been won'."

The exhibition covered some of Norway's history, its social and democratic development before the Germans invaded, architectural and cultural achievements, Viking art, its people and landscape. Mr. Olav Hindahl, writing on 13th October to thank the Lord Mayor said "I thoroughly enjoyed visiting your attractive city, and meeting the various local authorities. The exhibition was in my opinion excellent, and I am sure it will be most successful. The Museum was charming, and the rooms given over to the exhibition were just what one could wish. Please give my regards to Mrs. Cleveland and your daughter, and once more accept my best thanks for a most enjoyable visit, which I hope to have the pleasure of repeating."

During 1943 more Americans began to arrive in East Anglia as the number of airfields for the USAAF grew - some taken over from the RAF, others they built themselves. On arrival in this country men were confined to their base for the first month, then a little time off per week was allowed, and they took in the local villages and towns, going to pubs, dance halls, and cinemas.

"The arrival of American troops in our country has naturally aroused in us the desire to extend to them all the hospitality we can" said the Lord Mayor in a letter published in the *Eastern Daily Press* on Saturday 16th October. Calling for all to help towards their recreational and social needs, Arthur Cleveland said "Organised athletics, games, concerts, dances, lectures, etc., are being arranged as well as facilities for private hospitality. It is hoped by these means not only to relieve the loneliness which must of necessity affect those far from their native land, but also to give to both our visitors and ourselves a closer understanding of the others' outlook on life and so, by getting to know each other, establish a friendship which will have an important influence on the solution of the many problems which await the world."

The leader column writer of the *Eastern Daily Press* on the same day felt that "The Lord Mayor of Norwich expresses what we all feel as to our duty of full hospitality to the American troops who, in the pursuance of the great adventure of saving civilisation in which we are partners together, are now stationed in this country."

E.D.P. 16.10.43.

Our U.S. Visitors

Sir—The arrival of American troops in our country has naturally aroused in us the desire to extend to them all the hospitality we can.

Four years of war restrictions have made it impossible for us to do all we should like to, but during the last twelve months we have tried our best and with, I think it can be said, a considerable measure of success.

In the summer of last year the Lord Mayor (Alderman J. H. Barnes) called a committee representative of various interests in the city and county to see what provision we could make for the entertainment of our visitors, especially with regard to private hospitality.

Much was done in conjunction with the American Red Cross, and both from that society and the American troops themselves many expressions of their appreciation of our efforts have been received. Other organisations such as the Y.M.C.A., the Salvation Army, the Women's Voluntary Services, etc., have independently arranged entertainments which have proved of great value.

During the last few months the position has changed considerably. The American Army authorities have appointed special officers to deal with the welfare and recreations of their men and we have a small committee working in conjunction with them and the American Red Cross on the general principle that they will state their needs and we will assist in meeting them.

Organised athletics, games, concerts, dances, lectures, etc., are being arranged as well as facilities for private hospitality, and Mr. J. H. Westmacott, of the Ministry of Information, who has an office at the City Hall, is acting as liaison officer.

It is hoped by these means not only to relieve the sense of loneliness which must of necessity affect those far from their native land, but also to give to both our visitors and ourselves a closer understanding of the others' outlook on life and so, by getting to know each other, establish a friendship which will have an important influence on the solution of the many problems which await the world.

All of us can assist in this task and offers of help will be gratefully received, and if addressed to Mr. Westmacott at the City Hall will be transmitted to the proper quarters.—Yours faithfully,

ARTHUR J. CLEVELAND,
Lord Mayor.
City Hall, Norwich.
October 13th.

This letter, which was published in the Eastern Daily Press *on Saturday16th October, was from the Lord Mayor calling for everyone to do what they could to welcome, help, join in and become friends with Americans newly based in Norfolk.*

One of the sights of Norwich used to be the arrival in the horse drawn civic coach of the judge attending the Assizes Courts where the most serious cases of Norwich and Norfolk were heard by a senior judge [county Assizes were replaced in 1971 by Crown Courts]. At the autumn 1943 Assizes Justice Atkinson arrived at the cathedral on Sunday 17th October for the special service accompanied, as this was a ceremonial occasion, by the Lord Mayor, the Sheriff, the Deputy Lord Mayor, the Town Clerk, the Norwich Chief Constable, and members of the Council and City Bench. "The sermon was preached by the High Sheriff's Chaplain, the Rev. L. J. Baggott, who expressed the hope that the service, symbolising the historical association of Church and State, would always be held at Assize time" reported the local paper.

Evelyn Cleveland, the Lady Mayoress, was at the Citadel in St Giles on Sunday 25th October when Colonel Mary Booth, granddaughter of the Salvation Army founder, William Booth, gave a talk about her experiences of helping the people when she was in charge of Salvation Army work in Belgium. She recounted that, when war broke out and the government was removed with the Gestapo taking over, people began to flee. She said "the Salvation Army stayed on doing what they could but eventually had to get out and a permit was arranged for them to use the route of the retreating British Army." She described how they came to the bridge which was to be destroyed after their passage. "Suddenly I felt I could not go. I thought of all those refugees I had left behind in Brussels." She went back but was soon imprisoned. She talked about her experiences in an internment camp. "There were moments when I thought I would never again see those things I held dear. The Gestapo said 'Mary Booth need not think she will ever get out. We will hold on to her till the end'."

Eventually rescue came. "In the blackness of our night our eyes were fixed on the star of hope. We knew they would reach us if they could, and reach us they did. On behalf of my fellow prisoners and myself I do thank the Red Cross." Over a thousand people crowded into the Citadel to listen to Mary Booth, who had specifically asked for representatives of the Red Cross and Order of St. John to be there.

The Lord Mayor presided over the Norwich City Council meeting on Tuesday 2nd November when one of the items was the announcement of the new Chief Constable for Norwich, Alan Plume, who was to take over from John Henry Dain on his retirement at the end of the year. [John Dain was Chief Constable of Norwich City Police - the Chief Constable for Norfolk being Stephen Van Neck between 1928 and 1956. In 1968 Norwich City and Norfolk Constabularies combined to form the Norfolk Joint Constabulary].

The Lord Mayor welcomed Chief Inspector Alan Plume saying "In the government of this city there is no official who comes more into contact with all members of the community than does the Chief Constable. When I read the list of candidates selected for interview I felt that only a very good man could be the best of the lot and the impression I have now is that we have chosen well."

Alan Frederick Plume, from the Norfolk village of Colkirk, had been with the Metropolitan Police since 1920, and from August 1939 Chief Inspector of Whitehall Division with the added responsibilities for all police arrangements in connection with numerous state and ceremonial functions including the Houses of Parliament and Windsor Castle. Mr. Plume took up his new job in Norwich at the end of 1943.

CHIEF INSPECTOR PLUME

Alan Plume was announced at Norwich City Council meeting on the 2nd November to be the next Chief Constable of Norwich City Police, succeeding John Dain who was to retire at the end of the year.

Dr. Cleveland continued his desire to help visitors – particularly Americans. The *Eastern Daily Press* printed on Wednesday 3rd November an open letter from the Lord Mayor in which he said "As chairman of the committee for fostering good relations with members of the American Forces in our midst, I would make an appeal for help in a particular field. It is felt that much could be done in helping our guests to know Norfolk through visits to such places as buildings of historic interest, village churches, and local industrial undertakings. In every town and village there is certain to be at least one person who, by previous arrangement, would be willing to help Americans to appreciate the buildings of special interest by acting as guides, at the same time giving an informal chat to these men during leave periods." People interested in helping voluntarily were to contact a Mr. Westmacott in Room 320, Norwich City Hall.

With Americans stationed in many parts of Norfolk, they soon became part of the regions life. "All the time they were in Norfolk" Arthur Cleveland wrote after the war, "American soldiers were most generous to the hospital. The collecting box held by the wooden figure of a kilted Scotsman outside Millers, the tobacconists in London Street [No. 37, almost opposite Boots the Chemist], was a favourite receptable for their gifts. Two of their donations merit special notice. In November 1943, dollar bills to the value of £106 were placed anonymously in the box attached to the railings fronting St. Stephen's Road [outside the hospital in fact], and in the same month Sergeant G. W. Scott, of the United States Army Air Force, gave £28 5s 6d. in American currency. It was with great regret that we heard soon after of the death in air combat of this gallant friend."

Blackfriars Hall, next to St. Andrews Hall, was taken over by the Special Service Department of the American Air Force as a recreational centre for American servicemen visiting the city. Facilities for concerts, dancing, film shows, boxing etc. were available, as well as the hall being used as a base for other organised sports such as American football and basketball. The Lord Mayor went to Blackfriars Hall on Thursday 4th November to give to the Special Service Officer in charge two silver cups to be competed for in the athletic events. It was hoped that one of the cups could be for the winners of the football league.

In St. Andrews Hall on Friday 5th November the Lord Mayor accompanied by Evelyn Cleveland and the Sheriff John Brooksbank, welcomed back to Norwich six men repatriated from prisoner of war camps. A lunch was organised by Miss F. W. Burton of the W.V.S. and Miss Barnard, secretary of the Services Club. The men were Able-Seaman C. J. Harrell of Reepham Road, Hellesdon, who had been released from an Italian camp; Sergeant. A. R. Mason of the RAF of Bishops Bridge Road; Gunner F. E. Toy of Pottergate and Driver C. Crutchley of Beecheno Road both of the Royal Artillery; Pte. Ernest Cranmer of Bowers Avenue and Bandsman T. W. Bloxham of Belmore Road, both of the Royal Norfolk Regiment. Each man was greeted individually by the Lord Mayor, the Lady Mayoress and the Sheriff, and "given a hearty welcome back to the city" said the *Norwich Mercury*, a weekly newspaper published by the Norfolk News Company.

The next day, Saturday 6th November, the Lady Mayoress attended the Annual Meeting of the Norfolk Girl Guides at the Y.W.C.A. where the Chief Guide Commissioner for England, Lady Cochrane, congratulated the Norfolk Guides on their splendid efforts in connexion with the Baden-Powell Fund. She said "It is not always easy to know what our duty is, but I should like you to know that your work is a vital contribution to the nation's war effort."

NORWICH
PUBLICITY ASSOCIATION

PRESIDENT: THE LORD MAYOR.
CHAIRMAN: H. P. GOWEN, Esq., O.B.E., J.P.
VICE-CHAIRMAN: P. W. JEWSON, Esq., M.P., J.P.

What—you may perhaps ask—is the Norwich Publicity Association doing in these difficult times ?

Firstly it is helping many wives and families to find periodical accommodation near their Service men in the city. *Secondly* it is co-operating with the Army Educational Authorities in supplying historical material and information to Service Centres. *Thirdly* through its Offical Guide it helps many Service men—British and Allied—to an appreciation of this old city. *Fourthly* it maintains a lively correspondence with enquiries from many parts of our island. *Fifthly* it publishes a Fixture List of the events of the month in the city. All this is good investment in the interests of publicity for Norwich.

We can help you by your helping us.

THE BRIDEWELL
NORWICH

Telephone: 22233, Ex. 34

The Norwich Publicity Association was also quietly accumulating funds to publicise the City of Norwich after the war ended.

Lady Cochrane presented First Class badges to eleven guides, and home emergency service armlets to the same number of Rangers. Lady Preston, Divisional Commissioner for East Norfolk, proposed a vote of thanks, which was "seconded by the Great Brown Owl, Mrs. Brian Smith."

That Saturday night was not to be quiet, for between 10.30pm and midnight enemy aircraft flew over Norwich and dropped a few high explosive bombs, though luckily not much damage was done as they fell mainly on open ground. However some incendiary bombs landed in the Unthank Road to College Road area starting a number of fires. One man was slightly hurt. Arthur Cleveland writing after the war classed these as "minor raids." This he said was the last attack on the city. "After that, until the end of 1944, we were often called from our beds [he had a concrete bunker in the back garden] chiefly on account of the 'flying bombs'.

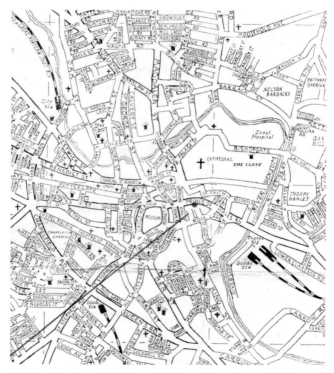

The line leading to the dot on this map of Norwich points to Taylor and Lovick, Estate Agents at 3 Prince of Wales Road. The company sponsored the map c1947. It is not known what the square blobs with spikes are - possibly schools. The crosses are churches.

"Fortunately the small number of these and of the unheralded 'rocket bombs' which reached Norfolk, fell in open country without doing much harm."

The raid did not stop the Remembrance Day arrangements the next morning - Sunday 7th November. Just before 10 o'clock wreaths were laid at the War Memorial at the back of the Market Place; then at 10am in the City Hall car park, various units assembled ready to march to the Cathedral. The parade was headed by members of the British Legion, followed by the band of the Royal Norfolk Veterans Association; the Air Training Corps; the Norfolk Fire Service, Fitness For Servicemen Association; Red Cross; St. John Ambulance Brigade; the Royal Observer Corps and the Air Raid Precautions Services.

The Lord Mayor and Lady Mayoress were at the Remembrance Day service in the Cathedral which was also attended by Sheriff John Brooksbank, the Town Clerk Bernard Storey and the Chief Constable of Norfolk Stephen Van Neck.

That was about the last of the mayoral year official engagements for Lord Mayor Cleveland and his officials, though he and the Lady Mayoress were at the Theatre Royal that Sunday evening where a full house listened to the Norwich Philharmonic Orchestra conducted by the cathedral organist Dr. Heathcote Statham. "With the inclusion of a number of Service players and the recruitment of some of the city's more youthful players, particularly in the string section, the orchestra, which filled the stage, may justly claim to have reached symphonic proportions. Early in the opening number, Elgar's sonorous transcription of Handel's Overture in D minor, it was evident that one was listening to an enthusiastic, very well drilled and arduously rehearsed body of musicians. Taken as a whole, the full orchestral effect was good." Also on the programme was the pianist "Eileen Joyce playing Rachmaninoff's tuneful Pianoforte Concerto in C minor" reported the *Eastern Daily Press*.

Dr. Cleveland, for the last time, on Monday 8th November, presided over the beginning of the Norwich City Council meeting, but the day was really for the incoming Mayor - William Finch, who was ceremonially installed as the new Lord Mayor of Norwich for the next twelve months. William Finch came to Norwich at the age of five, and went to Angel Road School. He spent most of his working life on the railways finishing up as Station Master and Goods Agent at the M&GN City Station - which then existed between Barn Road and Oak Street. Finch became a Labour Councillor in 1933, and was Sheriff in 1940. The new Sheriff for 1943-1944 was to be Norwich accountant, Roland Larking.

Norwich City Council "accorded a hearty vote of thanks to the outgoing Lord Mayor and Lady Mayoress on the motion of Mr. H. E. Witard, seconded by Mr. E. F. Williamson, both of whom eulogised the services of Dr. and Mrs. Cleveland in a time of extreme danger and difficulty" reported the *Eastern Daily Press*. "Responding, Dr. Cleveland acknowledged the friendliness sympathy and co-operation shown him by members and officials of the council, 'especially my comrade in chains, the outgoing Sheriff'."

1944 was quieter for the City of Norwich for it was not attacked again and no more damage was done or people injured or killed by enemy action. The war in Europe ended at midnight of Tuesday May 8th 1945, or to be precise, at one minute past the hour early the next morning.

CENTRAL HOSPITAL C.H.S.S. SUPPLY SERVICE

THE WAR ORGANISATION OF
THE BRITISH RED CROSS SOCIETY & ORDER OF ST. JOHN

Presented to *Mrs Cleveland*

in recognition of valuable services rendered in the making
of hospital supplies, during the world war from 1939

President

*This certificate awarded to Evelyn Cleveland for her work during the war is not
dated, so it is unknown when the presentation took place.*

Evelyn and Arthur Cleveland outside No.34 The Close.

After the War

Dr. Arthur Cleveland ceased being chairman of the Board of Management of the Norfolk and Norwich Hospital on 1st May 1943, and was elected a Vice-President that year. His Mayoral duties ended on 8th November. He was now 71 years old.

Although now retired, Arthur John Cleveland was not idle. He still did private medicals for the Norwich Union etc., which were carried out at his home in The Close. He started working on a history of the hospital which was to take over from where Sir Peter Eade's book *The Norfolk and Norwich Hospital 1770-1900* left off. The result was *A History of the Norfolk and Norwich Hospital 1900-1946* published by Jarrolds of Norwich in 1948. As he said, "I can claim to speak with a certain amount of authority, for during nearly all the period under review I was a member of the Medical Staff and Board of Management."

He looked back at what the war had done to Norwich. "Considering the structural devastation caused by the raiders, the numbers of killed and seriously wounded were surprisingly small. Of 30,354 dwelling houses in the city 2,082 were destroyed, 2,651 seriously damaged, and 25,621 moderately or slightly damaged. In addition shops and factories suffered severely. Yet the total fatal casualties in the city during the whole war were only 340 and, of the 1,092 injured, only 401 required admission to hospital. The reason for the dis-proportion between damage to buildings and loss of life was that the former was in great measure caused by incendiaries, which gave people time to get out of their houses, and the latter by high explosive bombs whose affect were instantaneous.

"The proportion of wounded requiring hospital treatment to killed – 401 to 340 – which agreed with the experience of other towns, was lower than most of us expected, and it was a cause for thankfulness that the provision very properly made exceeded the actual need."

The latter 1940s were a time of change, particularly regarding the nation's health and hospitals services. The voluntary hospital system, where subscribers had paid an annual amount, and money was raised by all kinds of fund raising methods, along with the consulting medical staff giving their services free, was about to change. Dr. Cleveland wrote "Peace brought to the Norfolk and Norwich, as to all our hospital services, greater problems than had war, and the future called for anxious thought and counsel. That the State must take a leading part in a new order was made imperative by financial considerations alone, for rising costs especially of salaries and wages [for staff] and the ever increasing calls on our work could not be met by the old methods.

"Must the voluntary system pass completely away, or could it be incorporated in the new order? Many clung to the hope that the latter alternative was possible, and when we read the high praise of the Norfolk and Norwich given in the Hospital Survey of the Eastern Area, published in May 1945, we felt we had justification for the belief that the old should be changed and not entirely replaced.

"In that conviction a joint appeal for £400,000 was issued at the beginning of 1945 by all the voluntary hospitals of Norfolk to enable them to make up for the lost years of war and to equip themselves for the increasing work before them.

"The return of a large Labour Party majority by the Parliamentary election of July 1945 indicated clearly that the voluntary system was dead and that, while the Norfolk and Norwich must continue to play an important part in the life of our county and city, it would be under a new flag and new masters. Would it still be inspired by the same spirit of service and hold the same place in the affections of those who turn to it for aid? Those of us who have spent many years of our lives in maintaining the traditions on which it was founded can only hope that it will, but we must be excused if we turn our gaze regretfully to its past."

The National Health Service Act swung into operation on 5th July 1948, about the same time as Arthur Cleveland's *A History of the Norfolk and Norwich Hospital 1900-1946* was published.

Dr. Arthur Cleveland's 1948 book about the Hospital.

A History of the
Norfolk and Norwich Hospital
from 1900 to the end of 1946

BY

ARTHUR J. CLEVELAND
O.B.E., M.D., F.R.C.P.

CONSULTING PHYSICIAN TO THE HOSPITAL
AND EX-CHAIRMAN OF THE BOARD OF MANAGEMENT

1948
JARROLD & SONS LTD.
NORWICH

Dr. Arthur John Cleveland did not give up his life's work as a medical man completely after 1948. A Group Management Committee came into operation with the new Health Service and Cleveland became a member. He also continued his private medical work throughout the1950s. According to Anthony Batty Shaw in his *Norfolk and Norwich Hospital Lives of The Medical Staff* published in 1971 "He continued his insurance work until a short time before his death in 1957." Arthur Cleveland died in St. Helen's Hospital in Bishopgate Street on 8th October aged 85. His wife Evelyn had died two years before - in September 1955.

On Thursday 15th December 1961 the British Medical Association 'presented two silver hand-wrought candelabra to Norwich Corporation' to commemorate 'the services of five members of the profession who have held office as Lord Mayor'.

The idea came from Dr. E. F. Claridge who had noticed that the legal profession had made a similar gift to Norwich of a silver salver a few years earlier. Dr. Branford Morgan, Senior Consulting Physician to the Norfolk and Norwich Hospital made the presentation at a reception at the City Hall saying he 'trusted future generations would admire them as examples of Norwich craftsmanship'.

The candelabra, bearing the city coat of arms and appropriate inscription, were made by Jack Neal in the workshop of silversmith Howard Brown at 50 The Close.

The *Eastern Daily Press* listed the Lord Mayors from the medical profession along with their year of service as 'Dr. J. G. Gordon-Munn (1914), Dr. G. S. Pope (1924), Dr. A. J. Cleveland (1942), Dr. I. D. Dickson (1955) and Mr. M. W. Bulman (1959)'.

The Norfolk and Norwich Hospital in 1946, after all damages repaired.

Norwich in 1955 - the sun shining on a flourishing city.

The Lower Close in Norwich. Arthur Cleveland and his wife lived in the middle house, No 33, for five years from 1931 to 1935, then moved in to No. 34, the house on the left, where they stayed through to the 1950s. Evelyn Cleveland died in 1955 and Arthur continued living there until 1957. Incidentally the house on the right, No. 32, an Officers Rest Home during part of the war, then became the home of Cleveland's daughter Deenie when she married Clare Van Neck, brother of Stephen Van Neck, just after the war. The houses were rented from the Dean and Chapter. Picture taken January 2020.

LORD MAYORS

1909	E. E. BLYTH
1910	Sir EUSTACE GURNEY Kt
1911	H. J. COPEMAN
1912	A. M. SAMUEL
1913	J. A. PORTER
1914	J. G. GORDON-MUNN
1915	E. B. SOUTHWELL
1916	G. M. CHAMBERLIN
1917	R. JEWSON
1918	Sir George M CHAMBERLIN Kt
1919	G. GREEN
1920	Lt-Col G. J. B. DUFF
1921	H. N. HOLMES
1922	Sir GEORGE H. MORSE Kt
1923	ETHEL M. COLMAN
1924	G. S. POPE
1925	T. GLOVER
1926	C. R. BIGNOLD
1927	H. E. WITARD
1928	H. P. GOWEN
1929	H. HARPER-SMITH
1930	MABEL M. CLARKSON
1931	Sir G. ERNEST WHITE Kt
1932	H. N. HOLMES
1933	F. C. JEX
1934	P. W. JEWSON
1935	W. A. RILEY
1936	H. FRAZER
1937	C. F. WATLING
1938	P. E. CURL
1939	J. F. HENDERSON
1940	B. J. HANLY
1941	J. H. BARNES
1942	A. J. CLEVELAND
1943	W. J. FINCH
1944	E. F. WILLIAMSON
1945	S. A. BAILEY
1946	W. O. COPEMAN
Nov 1947	W. G. CUTBUSH
May 1949	
1949	A. E. BAINES

Arthur Cleveland appears on this list of Lord Mayors in Norwich City Hall.

*The City Council often used names of past Mayors for new roads and streets.
Cleveland Road is possibly the shortest road in Norwich – running
between the Grapes Hill roundabout and St Giles Street.*

Some Sources

Catalogue of an Exhibition to Depict the History of the Hospital. A. Batty Shaw. 1971
East Anglia 1943. Douglas Brown. Terence Dalton Ltd. 1990
Five Generations of the Bignold Family. Sir Robert Bignold. Batsford. 1948
History of the Norfolk and Norwich Hospital 1900-1948. Arthur Cleveland. Jarrolds 1948
Leaf and the Tree. A. N. Holden and Co. for Boulton and Paul.1947
Mayors and Lord Mayors of Norwich 1836-1974. Patrick Palgrave-Moore. 1978
Norfolk and Norwich Hospital Annual Report for 1939.
Norfolk and Norwich Hospital Lives of The Medical Staff. Anthony Batty Shaw. 1971
Norfolk Events 1901-1938 & 1939-1950. Harold Jaffa. Norwich. 1950
Norwich - A Shattered City. Steve Snelling. Halsgrove, Somerset. 2012
Norwich Annual 1943. Roberts Printers, Norwich.
Norwich At War. Joan Banger. Poppyland Publishing.1989
Norwich Medico-Chirurgical Society. Antony Batty Shaw. 1967
Norwich Since 1550. Carole Rawcliffe and Richard Wilson. Hambledon & London. 2004
Norwich The Ordeal of 1942. E. C. Le Grice. Soman Wherry Press, Norwich. No date.
Norwich Under Fire. George Swain. Jarrold and Sons. c1945

Index

Note: Arthur Cleveland is not listed in this Index as his name, variously written as Arthur John Cleveland, Arthur Cleveland, Dr. Cleveland, or just Cleveland, as well as Lord Mayor, occurs on virtually every page. His wife, Evelyn Cleveland, is listed in the Index.

A

B

I

J

K

L

N

W

X

Y

Z